the
BEAUTY
of
BEING

KAROLYNE ROBERTS

the BEAUTY *of* BEING

STRIVE LESS AND LIVE MORE WITH GOD AS YOUR GUIDE

W

WHITAKER
HOUSE

Note: This book is not intended to provide medical advice or to take the place of medical advice and treatment from your personal physician. Neither the publisher nor the author takes any responsibility for any possible consequences from any action taken by any person reading or following the information in this book. Always consult your physician or other qualified health care professional before undertaking any change in your physical regimen, whether fasting, diet, medications, or exercise.

THE BEAUTY OF BEING
Strive Less and Live More with God as Your Guide

karolyne.com

ISBN: 979-8-88769-447-4
eBook ISBN: 979-8-88769-448-1
Printed in the United States of America
© 2025 by Karolyne Roberts

Whitaker House
1030 Hunt Valley Circle
New Kensington, PA 15068
www.whitakerhouse.com

LC record available at https://lccn.loc.gov/2025016603
LC ebook record available at https://lccn.loc.gov/2025016604

1 2 3 4 5 6 7 8 9 10 11 ⨆ 32 31 30 29 28 27 26 25

CONTENTS

INTRODUCTION

"What do you want to be when you grow up?" Were you ever asked that question? Most likely, you were. From a young age, we are conditioned to look ahead to dream of what we could eventually become. Then, when we grow up, many of us look back at our childhood years, wondering how they went by so fast, despising the trenches of adulthood along with its many burdens and responsibilities. Have you ever had a moment when you thought, "I wonder what it'd be like to be a kid again?"

The sad reality is that at both stages, whether in childhood or adulthood, many of us seem to face a level of discontentment with our current circumstances. Oftentimes, there is a tempting pull to either look ahead to the future or look back at the past and wonder, *what if.*

What if I become this?

What if I do that?

Or...

What if I did this?

What if I was that?

Now I beg the question...

What if we let kids be kids, helping them to realize they are already living a dream?

What if we embraced the beauty of being, even while becoming?

Being content with your current stage in life, despite the pressure to look back or ahead.

Being yourself, despite living in an age of extreme competition and comparison.

Being in the moment, embracing life's experiences, and simply living.

Because I'm here to tell you that *being* is enough.

I'm here to tell you that being is beautiful.

The very fact that you are breathing and here today is a miracle in itself. You were fearfully and wonderfully made by a God who intricately and intimately crafted you before time was even a factor. Before God pressed the play button on your life, He knew you, and He created you in your mother's womb. Before your first breath, before the first minute of your life, your spirit was in the mind and heart of your heavenly Father, the Creator of the heavens and the earth. He knew you and brought you forth as His daughter before there was ever even an earthly mother or father, before your clock even started ticking. So why do we allow the pressure of time to define our worth? Why do we let the titles associated with each stage of this life define our identity?

I am here to tell you that you are more than just the titles you became or desire to become one day. You are more than just a
_____ (fill in the blank). Even if you never add another title to

your name, you are more than enough as *just a daughter*—a daughter of the King of Kings, a daughter of the Lord of Lords. No other title you'll ever have will come close or compare.

The beauty of your position as God's daughter is that you don't need to strive for it. Nor do you need to perform or prove yourself. You are *just* a daughter because you've been *justified* by grace through faith. It is not of ourselves or our works; it is simply a gift of God, freely given so that no one can boast. (See Ephesians 2:8–9.) You are *just a daughter* because of the price God paid for you when He sent His one and only Son, Jesus Christ, to die for your sins on the cross.

Can you believe that?

Because God sacrificed His one and only Son, you can now reclaim your rightful place as *His* daughter. You don't have to work toward it. You don't have to look back at it and wish you had it. It is here for the taking—right now! You just have to simply accept it and rest in your God-given identity as a blood-bought, chosen *daughter* of God.

I'm writing this book for the one who just wants to simply *be*. For the one tired of going through life performing, who wants to experience more authentic living. For the one who wants to move beyond the pressures and expectations and break free from the box she's allowed herself to be placed in. I am writing this book for the one who no longer wants to be seen as the expert but is embracing a new season and is ready to learn.

If you are ready to explore, create, and become a student of life again, then *The Beauty of Being* is for you. This book will help you navigate the battle in your mind that's keeping you stuck and hindering you from showing up authentically in every area of your life. I pray that through this book, God brings your self-sabotage and negative self-talk to an end. Most importantly, I pray that it will give you the tools to walk in the freedom and victory that come from knowing your identity, embracing your personality, and living authentically.

If there is a constant tug-of-war between your desire to enjoy the moment and your dreams of having a successful future, I get it. Most people writing a book would say, "I was once where you were." But the truth is, I am there right now. Don't for a second think I have arrived.

We have a church culture that glorifies action and condemns inaction. I'm sure you have heard the following:

+ Actions speak louder than words.

+ Faith without works is dead.

+ Do what God has told you to do.

While those instructions may have a biblical foundation, we must use wisdom to understand they are not meant for every season or situation.

I've seen people cherry-pick Scriptures out of context as a way to pressure or coerce people into doing something. The truth is, most Scripture is best understood contextually and may sometimes only be applicable under certain conditions. Unfortunately, many people approach the Scriptures the same way they approach life: rushed, out of touch, and out of context. If we slowed down and really took the time to digest the Word of God, rather than just regurgitating popular Christian catchphrases, then we would have more than information and could step into the place of divine revelation, which can then lead to true transformation.

Many of us want change. We desire something sparkly and new that can make us feel special and productive—but at what cost? In the same way that we settle for surface-level information for the sake of superficial validation, we also handicap ourselves from going deeper in our walk with God because we keeping doing life on autopilot, going through the motions of church attendance and placing checkmarks in the boxes of our self-righteous affilia-tions. Unfortunately, our pompous view of Christianity that we strive to attain gives us a low grade in the eyes of God. According to James 1:27 (NLT), *"Pure and genuine religion in the sight of God the Father means caring for orphans and widows in their distress and refusing to let the world corrupt you."* Sadly, we've allow celebrity culture, politics, and elitism to enter the church.

God desires for us to do more than just sport the badge of a *Christian.* But since we've been so conditioned to find value in our titles, *Christian* is just another word we add to the list of things to which we belong because it makes us feel safe and a part of something. We like the feeling of connectivity that certain labels bring because we know there is a group of people attached to that name, and we want to feel seen, heard, and understood. Whether it's a Christian, mother, Republican, Democrat, teacher, minister, artist, barista, or anything else, everyone is looking to find their *tribe* and hopes that with these labels, their tribe will find them, like a little box of candy on the supermarket shelf just waiting to be discovered. The problem is, we attach our worth to who picks us up or who passes us by.

Yet Jesus already paid the price for you, so your value does not change despite what shelf of life you find yourself on, whether low or high, and despite your brand, label, or who stops to look or walk by.

Do you truly understand that you are a child of the King? God desires a deeper level of intimacy with you. While God cre-ated community and it is a much needed and beautiful thing, the connectivity you're truly seeking is not merely in the affiliations or groups you desire to be a part of. The connectivity you need first and foremost comes from God. He wants you to truly know Him, not just know *of* Him. The God of the universe wants an intimate relationship with you. He wants you to experience Him beyond the four walls of your church building, into the innermost chambers of your heart.

The biggest deficiency I have found with people who are struggling to believe—atheists, agnostics, humanists, and those who are deconstructing their beliefs—is that they lack a true encounter with the living God. That is often the one missing link. They went to church, they tried to do all the Christian things, they fell out in the spirit, and joined all the small groups, yet in all of that, they still struggled to find God. Why?

They were missing an encounter moment. Every true believer I know can pinpoint a moment when they encountered God. When that happens, you are never the same; it's like a straight head-on spiritual collision that changes you from the inside out. The only reason I am writing this book today is because I had an encounter with the God of the universe, my heavenly Father. Getting to know Jesus is the only way I truly came to know myself and who I am in Him. He is the one who has set me free from the bondage of people and the trenches of idolatry. Knowing God and having a true life-changing encounter with the Lord makes you more than just a Christian on paper; you become a disciple of Christ in real life.

I believe we sometimes miss moments and opportunities for encounter because we are in a distracted rush of *doing*. If you desire an encounter with God, I encourage you to linger a bit more in His presence. I used to sit in the balcony or in the back row of the church, next to the door, so I could be the first one out and in my car. I had social anxiety and was a spiritual babe in the faith. Now I linger. I worship a little longer. I'm not afraid to respond to the altar call if God is pulling on me to do so. This is the type of heart posture that is prepared and ready for an encounter with the Lord.

If you feel like your heart is hardened due to the cares of this life and it's hindering you from encountering God, pray this prayer: "Lord, please soften my heart. Remove any scales from my eyes. Help me to truly encounter You and experience You in a real and personal way. I want more of You, Jesus. Amen."

You will seek me and find me when you seek me with all your heart.   (Jeremiah 29:13)

I believe that slowing down and embracing the beauty of being opens you up to experiencing more of God's daily encounters and miracles in your life. Sometimes it's that quiet whisper from the Holy Spirit or the stillness in waiting on the Lord that usher in the greatest breakthroughs. We think the constant hustle is the key to our success, but if you don't slow down, you will accomplish less than you could if you had been more present in the moment and taken the time to simply be. Let me give you an example.

I was making a cake recipe for the first time. As you may know, with baking, when trying anything new and working with different types of ingredients, it's important to test the recipe first, taste it, and see if you can make any adjustments to improve upon it. The problem was, during my first time making this cake, I wanted to film the process so I could teach the recipe to others. So imagine me in the kitchen, doing something I'd never done before, while trying to arrange my camera and lights at different angles and trying to rush the process and complete it before the sun went down. It was quite literally a mess, flour and sugar everywhere!

And guess what? After all the filming, the cake came out gummy and flat. The recipe was off; I wasn't in the moment to really focus, learn, pay attention to the measurements, and give the cake what it really needed. Instead, I was trying to teach others how to replicate my disaster.

That's how it is for some of us. God has you in a new season where He wants you to simply be. He wants you to discover who you are in Him, not just your identity in Christ, but your own unique fingerprint and personality. It's okay if that evolves over time, just don't rush this season. Learn the special ingredients that make you, *you*. God is the ultimate baker, and if you surrender your life and this process to Him, you will end up with the best results. Don't be in a rush to teach; fully embrace this process and learn.

Maybe you are used to being in a position of authority. Maybe you are used to being perceived as a teacher, leader, or expert. If you are reading this book, I assume you feel this tug to simply *be* and you are transitioning into a new era of your life. This Scripture comes to mind:

> *Forget the former things; do not dwell on the past. See, I am doing a new thing! Now it springs up; do you not perceive it? I am making a way in the wilderness and streams in the waste-land.*   (Isaiah 43:18–19)

It may seem natural to try to cling to old ways of doing and operating. If it's what we have known for so long, it may be a source of comfort to us. We are familiar with our old persona, positions, and places.

But will you allow God to carry you through this awkward and vulnerable transition? Will you call Him to draw you out into the wilderness, where the only thing you can fall back on, the only thing you can rely on, is God Himself? In the wilderness, God wants to refresh you. He said He will provide *"streams in the waste-land."* You may think that in the wilderness, God is punishing you, has forgotten you, or has forsaken you. The truth is, just like the Israelites who came out of slavery, He's trying to give you a break from strenuous labor and bondage. He is delivering you but wants to refresh you before bringing you into the promised land. The wilderness is unfamiliar, strange territory. That's okay; explore, learn, and grow.

Allow the manna of the Lord to sustain you through this time. In Exodus 16:4, the Lord said to Moses, *"I will rain down bread from heaven for you. The people are to go out each day and gather enough for that day. In this way I will test them and see whether they will follow my instructions."* God provided for and sustained the Israelites during their journey in the wilderness with this bread from heaven, manna. This provision was also a test that came with a set of instructions.

Because I failed and wasn't present enough to effectively execute the cake recipe the first time, I had to learn from my mistakes and try again after learning how I could improve. Just like the Israelites in the wilderness, I had to go around the same mountain again. I'm thankful though because the second time around, I was able to bake the cake correctly because I gave it my complete focus and attention. When you are present and in the moment, you are more self-aware and conscious of your mistakes and how you can improve. When I baked the cake the second time, it came out just as it should.

In this age of social media and content creation, we are so eager and pressured to post, to push submit, to publish the content. Yet if not used in moderation, these tools can become crutches and distractions to our growth and learning process. It's a shame to be growing numerically in likes and followers on social media but stagnant in spiritual and personal growth. Phones and electronics are not allowed in most classrooms because they are distractions. It's hard for students to focus and learn anything when they are consumed with the tiny screens in front of them.

I learned my lesson with that cake. Now I practice and master a recipe first, then post later. Take a tip from me: Don't be in a rush to share. Bake the cake a few times before finalizing the recipe. Have those conversations with God first and pray about it a few times before publishing the video or blog post. The first few drafts should always be reserved for you and the Holy Spirit, not with the intention of aiming for perfection, but with the purpose of embracing the process. The finished product does not have to be proof that you're perfect, but it should be proof that you're present. *The beauty of being while becoming* is that you don't ever *arrive*, but you come to realize that God has always been there and wherever He is, that's where you should remain.

1

BEING WHILE BECOMING

It is the one thing we all have in common.

It is the fundamental thread that binds us all together.

It is our greatest weakness, while it is also a position of power.

It is our humanity.

It's a core identity that marks all of us, in good times and bad.

We are human *beings*.

The following Scripture affirms this:

*And He has made **from one blood every nation of men** to dwell on all the face of the earth, and has determined their preappointed times and the boundaries of their dwellings, so that they should seek the Lord, in the hope that they might grope for Him and find Him, though He is not far from each one of us; for **in Him we live and move and have our being**,*

*as also some of your own poets have said, "For **we are also His***
offspring."   (Acts 17:26–28 nkjv)

This Scripture affirms the function and identity of all mankind. In Him, our function is to *"live and move and have our being."* We are human beings made in His image; we are His offspring.

Scripture also says, *"To all who did receive him, to those who believed in his name, he gave the right to become children of God"* (John 1:12).

So what does all this mean? Well, have you ever found yourself saying or heard someone confidently protest something with the words, "I'm human!" or "I'm only human." I know I have on several occasions. Whether I was apologetic about a mistake I made or overwhelmed with empathy toward someone who was suffering, the essence of my humanity is naturally evident.

God created humanity, also known as mankind, in His own image.

In the very beginning, *"God created mankind in his own image, in the image of God he created them; male and female he created them"* (Genesis 1:27).

GOD THOUGHT OF YOU LONG AGO

Have you paused to think that we are the group of *them* referred to from the beginning of time? You have probably heard it taught that God has a plan for you and knew you before you were formed in your mother's womb. (See Jeremiah 1:5.) That in itself is a remarkable fact. Yet have you considered rewinding just a bit further? Let's go way back, prior to your natural conception. God had you in mind before the earth's creation. God didn't just know you before you were formed in your mother's womb; God knew you before your mother even had a womb, or before her mother's mother had one. God knew you before He even formed the foundations of the earth. From day one, He had an image of who you would be. You are made in His image—the image of the almighty God.

We are all human *beings* and in essence the most beloved form of natural life, engrafted from the hands of the great I AM. (See Exodus 3:14.)

> *But there is a place where someone has testified: "What is mankind that you are mindful of them, a son of man that you care for him? You made them a little lower than the angels; you crowned them with glory and honor and put everything under their feet."* (Hebrews 2:6–8)

No other form of creation has experienced the expression of love as we have from God the Father. Jesus didn't come to die and sacrifice His life for the animals. He came to die and sacrifice His life for us. Angels don't get to be seated with Christ *"in the heavenly places"* (Ephesians 2:6 NKJV), but we do.

Though both human beings and animals will return to dust, we do not share the same experience in life. The Bible talks about three different types of living organisms on this earth:

+ **Living creatures:** Wild animals, livestock, small animals, fish in the sea, and birds in the sky. (See Genesis 1:25–26.)
+ **Human beings:** Male and female. (See Genesis 1:27.)
+ **Heavenly hosts:** Cherubim, angels, seraphim, and archangels. (See Genesis 3:24; 16:7; Isaiah 6:2–7; Psalm 148:2; 1 Thessalonians 4:16.)

OUR FUNCTION AS HUMAN BEINGS

Each of these groups has a different function, and today I specifically want to break down our function as human *beings*, but before we do that, I want to define the word *function* first.

Function can be defined as "the action for which a person or thing is specially fitted or used or for which a thing exists."[1]

The Greek word for *function* is *práksis*, which is defined as "a doing, a mode of acting; a deed, act, transaction."[2]

This is important to note because throughout this book, I will be discussing themes of performance, action, busyness, and the like.

I think it's essential to break down these concepts so that you'll be able to distinguish vain activity from a purpose-driven lifestyle. They are two completely different things. Vanity is one of the pitfalls of going through life without a clear sense of purpose.

One of the clear purposes that God has for us on the earth is to simply enjoy life, His creation, and our work on this earth in serving Him. Enjoyment is key to the *beauty* of being, and it contains the root word "joy," which we know only comes from the Lord.

The wise King Solomon breaks this concept down even more, saying:

> *I also said to myself,* "As for humans, God tests them so that they may see that they are like the animals. Surely **the fate of human beings is like that of the animals;** the same fate awaits them both: **As one dies, so dies the other.** All have the same breath; humans have no advantage over animals. Everything is meaningless. All go to the same place; all come from dust, and to dust all return. Who knows if the human spirit rises upward and if the spirit of the animal goes down into the earth?" So I saw that **there is nothing better for a person than to enjoy their work, because that is their lot.**

---

1. *Merriam-Webster Dictionary*, s.v. "Function," www.merriam-webster.com/dictionary/function.
2. G4234. práksis. *Strong's Greek Concordance.*

For who can bring them to see what will happen after them?
(Ecclesiastes 3:18–22)

If you heard this discourse for the first time, not knowing the person speaking those words, would you believe it came from a king? In fact, these words were spoken by the wisest king who ever lived, King Solomon, the one who had it all—the wealth, the riches, the experiences, and many wives. He is the one saying, *"Everything is meaningless."* These words carry weight because they are coming from someone who was high-achieving and high-performing. This message would not be the same if it came from someone who has naturally despised the idea of wealth or someone content with living a plain, quiet life. King Solomon is essentially saying, "I have seen it all, and our fate is still no better than that of animals."

Although both people and animals return to dust, God promises that believers will be redeemed and given new bodies once Christ returns. The Bible does not state that animals will receive regenerated bodies in the second coming as we will. (See 2 Corinthians 5:4.)

One of the greatest takeaways from the wisdom of King Solomon in Scripture is, *"There is nothing better for a person than to enjoy their work, because that is their lot"* (Ecclesiastes 3:22). Yet so many people are not even sure how to apply this to their own lives. They are not sure how to truly rest, enjoy their work, and simply be. I believe that there is a greater level of enjoyment that God calls us to and it's more than momentary fun or the fleeting pleasures of this life. It's a soul-deep joy infused with the presence of the Holy Spirit. It's the type of joy that will not only carry you through, but it will cause you to shine even in the darkest of times. So then, how can we truly experience joy in its fullness while being surrounded with so much vanity on this earth?

The greatest joy does not come from pursuing pleasure or prominence, but rather from experiencing God as we carry out our purpose. Have you ever heard the saying, "Do what you love and you will never have to work a day in your life?" It's true. Toiling and working just for the next paycheck or promotion can buy you a meal at a five-star restaurant, but once you've digested the food, you are left with a heart that is bankrupt and void of any true joy and fulfillment. Many of us are often waiting for the next high and mountaintop experience, the next holiday or vacation that we have been looking forward to all year, the next business launch, or the next thing that we think will finally make us happy. But once all the confetti has fallen and the balloons deflate, we find ourselves back in the same mundane place, grasping after the next blow of the wind.

When you slow down and embrace the beauty of being, it causes you to be more purpose-conscious and intentional. When you're walking in your purpose daily, success is no longer a goal, metric, or standard you seek to reach attain. Rather, success is the joy and peace you feel when you are divinely aligned and in daily partnership and communion with the Father. Therein is the difference between us and the animals; God chooses to partner with us to do His will and through this communion with the Father, Jesus, and the Holy Spirit, we get to experience a life of true fulfillment and enjoyment, not because of what we have, but because of who we know. We get the privilege, honor, and pleasure of working with God; the animals don't. The Bible says in 1 Corinthians 3:9 (NKJV), "*For we are God's fellow workers; you are God's field, you are God's building.*"

Animals need the instinct of survival in their world of predator versus prey, but as human beings, we are not just living to survive; God also gives us assignment, purpose, calling, and more. God gave us dominion and authority over the animals, but He also gave us specific reasons for being.

Then God blessed them, and God said to them, "Be fruitful and multiply; fill the earth and subdue it; have dominion over the fish of the sea, over the birds of the air, and over every living thing that moves on the earth." (Genesis 1:28 NKJV)

THE GREATEST GIFT

Lastly, we can't forget the most important gift that God gave to us humans, and that is the gift of His one and only Son, Jesus Christ, and the gift of salvation and everlasting life. You don't have to go through life striving when you were created to thrive. Jesus broke the curse of sin and He came so we can have life and *"have it more abundantly"* (John 10:10 NKJV).

I want to talk a little more about the function we all play in the biosphere of creation. Believe it or not, the function of each group is plainly hidden in each name. For instance, our function as humans is to simply live and *be*. That is why we are called human *beings*, and not human *doings*. The function of heavenly hosts is to *host* and serve God, which also means war as an army because God's angels fight on our behalf. Then finally, the function of living creatures is to live and constantly contend for the survival of themselves and their offspring, whether they are predator or prey. And the blood of these animals carries the life-force and energy that most living organisms feed from on the food chain.

Our function comes out of our identity, not the other way around. You are not what you do, but you do from who you are. Animals are living creatures, so they must live. We are human beings, so we must be. Many people in the world go out and look for things that they can do—such as finding jobs, opportunities, projects, etc.—in hopes that from performing these duties, they will find identity. The truth is, you were already given an identity from the foundations of this earth, and if you know who you are, you will no longer need to function by performing your way through life, but rather, you can experience the beauty in simply being.

As I said from the start of this chapter, we all have one thing in common as humans, and that is the same red blood running through our veins and the same function to which the Father has called us.

In the world's eyes, our function most often has to do with our performance or our job title. Maybe you can relate to meeting someone for the first time and having them ask you, "What do you do?" or perhaps you asked them that question. Generally, the first thing that many people want to know when they meet a person is their function in life. Why? Well, often it's because people want to know what you can do for them. But you may recall that the biblical definition of function is quite different. It is less of a temporary performance and more of an ongoing mode of action. The words used to describe "function" from a biblical stance are more experiential in nature, such as the word *doing*. On the other hand, the words used to describe "function" from a worldly standpoint are more positional in nature, such as the word *calling*.

WORLDLY FUNCTION VS. BIBLICAL FUNCTION

I have created a simple chart to clearly put this concept into perspective.

Worldly Definition of Function	Biblical Definition of Function (Greek)
Keywords: Duty, office, calling, performance	Keywords: A doing, mode of action
Part(s) of speech: Common nouns referring to roles or titles	Part(s) of speech: Verbal nouns; verbs that function as nouns (gerunds)
Nature: Positional i.e. job titles	Nature: Experiential i.e. experiences
Examples: Mom Wife Author Minister Intercessor	Examples: Raising children Homemaking Writing Ministering Praying and fasting

From this chart, you can compare and contrast the two different perspectives on function. Keep these ideas in mind as I continue to address this topic. Now, let's look at this practically. Many of us have used the word "function" in our day-to-day lives. For example, have you ever said, "I can't function without coffee," or "I can't function without sleep," or something similar?

In this sense of the word, we are saying we can't perform well or meet our day-to-day duties without those things. When we make statements like this, it is coming from the worldly perspective of what it means to function; it's coming from a performative place. When we feel like we've fallen short of functioning in the way we expect, it directly takes a shot at our identity because from the worldly perspective, your duty or function is directly linked to your role or title. This type of thinking, as you might expect, leaves loopholes and opens doors for the enemy to have a field day in our minds and beat at our self-esteem.

If you feel like you can't execute your motherly duties well, you might be tempted to label yourself as a bad mom. Or if you feel like you can't perform well enough to reach your ambitious goals, you may fall into the trap of labeling yourself as a failure when the Bible has already declared you as a victor. (See 1 John 5:4.)

The Word of God says, "*Don't copy the behavior and customs of this world, but let God transform you into a new person by changing the way you think. Then you will learn to know God's will for you, which is good and pleasing and perfect*" (Romans 12:2 NLT)

We are not called to function or think of functioning in the way that the world does. We are called to renew our mind with the Word of God. That is why I broke down the word "function" while comparing its definitions and doing a deep dive into its true meanings and origin.

If we change our mind about what it means to function and acknowledge it as an experience rather than a role or title, we will be more apt to live the abundant life that Jesus desires for us to have and truly be who God has created us to be outside of temporary, shifting positions.

ENJOYMENT AND EXPERIENCE

There are two keys to the beauty of being: enjoyment and experience. We gently touched on both of these key concepts earlier, but now I want to dive a little deeper. First, we need to stop functioning out of duty and instead start to function out of experience. There are so many beautiful moments that God wants you to experience as you walk with Him through life, but if you are more focused on the results than you are on the journey, you will miss out on the best part.

Many of our societies are results-driven. They are focused on the likes, the followers, the awards, the accolades, the money, the fame ... but what about the experience? What about the encounters that God wants to have with you throughout the journey? What about the things that God wants to show you and teach you throughout the process?

The beauty of being is recognizing that though you are physically on this earth, you *"are not of the world"* (John 17:16). We do not have to subscribe to the world's ideologies and follow the world's ways. We are of a different nature, a spiritual nature. Before we are human beings, we are spiritual beings. We may be physically on this earth but we are spiritual in the Lord and we are *of* God. We are children of God, made in His image, whose only true function and duty is to *be*. True being looks like abiding in Him. It looks like dwelling in and clinging to God ever so tightly.

> *Therefore whoever humbles himself as this little child is the greatest in the kingdom of heaven.* (Matthew 18:4 NKJV)

Have you ever been told you need to *become* something in order to be great? The world has convinced many of us that we need to make something of ourselves when the truth is we just have to discover *who* we are made for. We were made in the image of God, but we are not God. A child has the same genetic makeup and reflects the features of his parents but still does not have the same position of authority as they do. Pride can get in the way when we try to play the role of God instead of accepting who God has already made us. That is why if we truly want to be great, we must humble ourselves as little children. When you become like a child and embrace your position as God's daughter, it frees you from being enslaved to the idol of self-achievement.

It was the pride of my desires of what I wanted to *become* and *do* in this life that drew me away from who God already called me to *be* and what God has already *done*. We must always remember that apart from God, we can *"do nothing"* (John 15:5). That is what Jesus tells us in the parable of the vine dresser in John 15. Jesus illustrates that we must abide in the vine in order to bear fruit. Yet wherever you find pride, it means you have ceased to abide. Maybe you were bearing fruit at the beginning. Maybe you started off your journey with God but then forgot that He was the one sustaining you. That is why we should remain humble and never forget where our help comes from.

God is our source. He is the vine, and as His daughters, we are the branches. Like a child who comes forth from their parents, we as spiritual children come forth in power from our God. If your fruit started off ripe yet has begun to wither, the culprit could be the poison of pride.

Even the mere consideration that we can accomplish anything without God is an open door for pride. Burnout is a form of falling due to pride. Burnout is evidence that we have allowed pride to seep into our hearts.

WHEN PRIDE IS DISGUISED

Pride often comes disguised and wrapped up in the form of false humility and acts of service, when the truth is, we are really just people pleasing or attempting to be "God-pleasing," but the only way to truly please God is through faith, not our works. In fact, *"without faith it is impossible to please God"* (Hebrews 11:6). We cannot please God without God's help, and we cannot please God without faith. The beauty of being is posturing yourself in the humility of a child dependent on the Father. God is calling us to have a childlike faith, knowing that as our Father, He will take care of our every need. His love for us is unconditional, and we can find rest depending on His faithfulness.

Sometimes, we allow pride to creep in because we try to take our desires into our own hands. I believe that pride is mismanaged ambition motivated by fear. There is nothing wrong with having desires; God will actually give us our desires, but we must first delight ourselves in Him. (See Psalm 37:4.) The problem is when you put more emphasis on your own efforts as a means to achieve a goal rather than on God's grace. The truth is, I am not self-made; I am God-made.

I can't take credit for the things I have achieved and accomplished because if it weren't for the breath God put in my lungs, I wouldn't be here today. If it weren't for the talent He gave me to begin with, I wouldn't have the opportunity to multiply it. He is the one who has gifted me and allowed these gifts to make room for me. He is the one who impregnated me and allowed me to be a mother. He is the one who graces me to be a wife. I could do nothing, absolutely nothing, without the grace of God in my life. This is not discouraging but actually encouraging when you recognize that God's got you and your success is not dependent on you. Yes, God needs your participation, but ultimately, it's His providence that will carry you through.

RESTING IN THE FATHER'S ARMS

One of my goals in writing this book is to relieve you of the heavy burdens that may be weighing on your chest. Rather, like a naked baby during the first few moments of life, I encourage you to lie skin-to-skin on the chest of your heavenly Father.

Breathe and rest like you have no cares in the world.

Some of us need to return to the childlike faith that we had when we were just saved, just like a newborn baby. All a baby does is rest and eat. All a baby does is allow the parent to carry them wherever they go; a baby is just a baby, fully reliant on their parent. God is calling you just a daughter. He is calling you to be fully reliant on Him. He is calling you back to the place you were before life got busy—before the ministry, the business, the family, and all the other blessings God gave you that somehow turned into idols.

God is calling you back to the routine of resting in Him and feasting on His Word. Resting and eating should be your greatest priorities in this season. Those activities alone will nourish you back to health as you allow the Father to carry you so you can renew your mind and learn how to walk again, how to talk again, and how to *be* again. You may be thinking, "Karolyne, I should be much further along in my spiritual walk. I can't be returning to the stage of being a babe in Christ. I thought I was more mature than this." The unfortunate truth is that some of us mistake longevity for maturity. Just because you have been saved for a considerable length of time does not equate to maturity. Furthermore, becoming mature doesn't mean you cease being God's baby. You are still His child, His daughter, no matter what season of life you find yourself in.

The other day, my daughter said to me, "Mommy, I think it's weird that you call Grandma 'mommy' because you're a grown-up." Then I had to explain to her that no matter how old I get in life, my mommy will always be my mommy, and I will always be her daughter. It's the same with God. I want you to know that even in your twenties, thirties, forties, fifties, sixties, and beyond, God still looks at you as His little girl. He adores you like you are one of His babies just born yesterday.

Remember, God's timing is not our timing. *"With the Lord a day is like a thousand years, and a thousand years are like a day"* (2 Peter 3:8). The span of our life is but a mist from His perspective. From your perspective, you may feel like you are growing old. You may feel like there is nothing to be excited about anymore. But that's far from the truth. God is excited for you and about you. He created you with a purpose and brought you to this world for His own great pleasure. (See Philippians 2:13.)

> *For the LORD your God is living among you. He is a mighty savior. He will take delight in you with gladness. With his love, he will calm all your fears. He will rejoice over you with joyful songs.* (Zephaniah 3:17 NLT)

So if you need a season to take a break and pause, if you have to take some time to rest, say no, and enjoy moments of simply being, then that's okay. As a matter of fact, it's more than okay; it's holy. It's more of God and less of you.

It's what I did after spending ten years of my life performing, resulting in burnout. I spent most of my twenties people-pleasing, thinking I was God-pleasing, until I finally crashed and came to the end of myself. From writing books to hosting conferences to building platforms, I did so much, and I thought I became so much because of the titles. Yet at the end of it all, I felt like Solomon and thought, "All this is meaningless. Simply vanity. Grasping for the wind." (See Ecclesiastes 1:14.) Then, on my thirtieth birthday, I welcomed a new era in my life and experienced the rebirth of my spiritual infancy. I resolved in my heart that I wanted to go beyond the shallow end of life and dive deeper into a greater dimension of my purpose and identity. Instead of being defined by what I could or could not do in my own flesh, I decided to rest in what Christ has already done through His great power and unconditional love for us.

GROWTH TAKES TIME

Many voices promote the idea of women *becoming*. While there is nothing inherently wrong with this message, something is essentially missing—our being. We have lost appreciation for what God has already done in us and our current circumstances. We have also forgotten that growth is a process that happens naturally over time. We have overlooked the beauty and wonder of divine simplicity. There is beauty in being even while becoming.

I pray I can help you embrace gratitude, slow down, and realize you have permission to simply *be*. The best version of yourself is not an idealistic vision of what you can eventually become after years of performance and promotion; it's simply resting in your grace-filled position as a daughter of God.

There is a journey that the Bible refers to when it comes to our personal and spiritual growth in Christ. Philippians 1:6 says, *"Being confident of this, that he who began a good work in you will carry it on to completion until the day of Christ Jesus."* This is the journey I'm referring to as *being while becoming*, a journey which is rooted in the redemptive work of the cross. From this verse, I think it's important to note that we are a work in progress, and God takes us through a sanctification *process*. Process is the key word here; we never just *arrive*. There are phases to this process. This Scripture says God *"began a good work"* not that He *finished* all the work in you. Clearly, we have a part to play in this too because the apostle Paul even admonishes the church by saying, *"Continue to work out your salvation with fear and trembling"* (Philippians 2:12). This daily walk is a marathon, not a sprint. The process has started, but it is incomplete. God is the one who will be faithful to carry out His work within us and bring it to a state of completion, but in the meantime, we must embrace the beauty of *being*.

JESUS GAVE US A MODEL TO FOLLOW

Jesus lays out the perfect example for us in the Bible. Before He uttered His last famous words on the cross, *"It is finished"* (John 19:30), He modeled the beauty of being while becoming, and He was becoming more than any one person could ever be or imagine. But in order to do that, He had to walk in the experience of a human *being*. He had been tempted as we have but never sinned. He went through the hardest experiences known and unknown to man, and that's what makes this redemption story so beautiful.

Jesus knows what it means to be in our shoes. He knows what it means to simply *be* a man on this earth. That is why He was able to become the Savior of the world. He is able to relate to each and every one of us and our struggles. Hebrews 4:15 (NLT) says, *"This High Priest of ours understands our weaknesses, for he faced all of the same testings we do, yet he did not sin."*

That's the beauty of being; you're able to relate to others and truly be there for them. There is a depth that comes with walking through certain trials and embracing various life experiences. It begets true authenticity. Recognizing the great value that can come from the process can help encourage those seeking contentment in their journey.

A lyric from a song by one of my favorite worship singers, Cece Winans, goes, "It wasn't easy, but it was worth it."[3]

The process that Jesus went through to get to the cross was not easy at all. It was hard, ugly, strenuous, crushing, intense, revealing, and more. Yet it is because Jesus's willingness to obey His Father through this dual process of being while becoming that we have the gift of salvation today. Jesus was willing to humble Himself and remain obedient to God while becoming a man to fulfill His purpose of redeeming mankind.

---

3. Cece Winans, "It Wasn't Easy," on *Alabaster Box* (WellSpring Gospel, 1999).

My question for you is, are you willing to *be* who God has made you to be while simultaneously becoming who your purpose calls you to be?

Your function is to *be*. But you are *called* to become. That is a process. To understand the beauty of being, you must be able to distinguish these two parallel modes of reality. Jesus knew this. He knew He was the Son of God. He knew He was I AM, but He understood that He had to walk through a certain process to become the Savior He was called to be and fulfill His ultimate purpose.

This was demonstrated when Jesus went to be baptized by John the Baptist. John knew who Jesus was, but what he didn't understand was that even for Jesus, a certain process was necessary.

> *Then Jesus came from Galilee to John at the Jordan to be baptized by him. And John tried to prevent Him, saying, "I need to be baptized by You, and are You coming to me?" But Jesus answered and said to him, "Permit it to be so now, for thus it is fitting for us to fulfill all righteousness." Then he allowed Him.*
> (Matthew 3:13–15 NKJV)

Jesus was saying, let it *be*. This must *be* in order to *become*. This thing must happen in order to fulfill all righteousness. This is a part of the process. This is a part of God's plan. Jesus is telling His cousin, John the Baptist, to be confident of this. We are called to have faith in the fact that God is faithful enough to finish what He started in us. If He is our beginning, then He is also our end. Remember, God *is* the Alpha and the Omega, the beginning and the end. If there is a being, there is always a becoming. The issue is many of us try to skip the beauty of being and arrive at becoming. We neglect the process and place more value on the end result. Yet the process is actually more significant than we think.

THE PROCESS OF BEING

Through the process of being, we are:

PREPARED

"You also must **be ready** all the time, for the Son of Man will come when least expected" (Luke 12:40 NLT).

PERFECTED

"But let patience have its **perfect** work, that you **may be perfect** and complete, lacking nothing" (James 1:4 NKJV).

PURIFIED

"Do everything without grumbling or arguing, so that you may **become** blameless and **pure,** 'children of God without fault in a warped and crooked generation.' Then you will shine among them like stars in the sky" (Philippians 2:14–15).

PROOFED

"And do not be conformed to this world, but be transformed by the renewing of your mind, that you may **prove** what is that good and acceptable and perfect will of God" (Romans 12:2 NKJV).

2

"JUST A DAUGHTER"

What is left of you when you pull back the layers and false sense of security that has covered you throughout the years? Who are you when the fig leaves finally fall off? Many of us hide behind the makeup, the titles, the works, and the busyness of life. Yet do you know your *true*, spiritual, genetic makeup? I am not talking about your culture, your skin color, or the ancestral ties you may have to an earthly kingdom. I am talking about your belonging to a heavenly kingdom, your blood-bought right, and your relation to the God of the universe.

When you start pulling back the layers that you thought would keep you safe, you realize that in your nakedness, in the humility of your humanity, you are closest to God and most in tune with yourself. A wise man once said, *"Naked I came from my mother's womb, and naked I will depart"* (Job 1:21). A child spends its preliminary moments with God before being born naked into this world. Then, upon the death of a person, naked they return to their Creator for all eternity. When Adam and Eve were first placed in the garden of Eden, they were naked. Yet when the sin of pride entered into their hearts, their eyes were opened, and they were ashamed. It is this shame that caused them to cover themselves with fig leaves and hide in fear from the Lord.

So if you find yourself hiding behind your own fig leaves, I beg you to ask yourself the questions, "What am I ashamed of?" and "Why am I afraid?" Also, consider what your fig leaves may be. They could be different for everyone. Maybe your fig leaves are the expensive designer clothes you wear because you grew up with the shame of poverty, feeling like you weren't enough. Or maybe your fig leaves are all of your degrees and accomplishments because you grew up never hearing the words, "I am proud of you" and you want to prove to yourself that you are worth being proud of. Maybe you fear embarrassment, failure, or what people have to think or say about you. So you put on these fleeting fig leaves because your fears cause you to run and hide in an attempt to cover the shame.

I am here to help you pull back all the layers, become confident in your true identity, and rest in the safety you have been desiring all along. Maybe you are fooling everyone else around you with your performance. Maybe you have the perfect smile, but behind it all, you are crying inside. You are hiding in plain sight, seemingly fooling everyone else, but you can never fool or hide from God. Adam and Eve hid from God with their fig leaves:

> *They suddenly felt shame at their nakedness. So they sewed fig leaves together to cover themselves. ... Then the LORD God called to the man, "Where are you?" He replied, "I heard you walking in the garden, so I hid. I was afraid because I was naked."* (Genesis 3:7, 9–10 NLT)

Adam and Eve were afraid of their nakedness. Due to pride, they were afraid of their humanity and sinful nature. So rather than running to God during the fall, they ran away from God. In their weakness, fear, and pride, they thought they could hide and outsmart God with their fig leaves.

REMOVING THE FIG LEAVES

After finally peeling back all the layers, are you afraid of what's left? Are you afraid of your nakedness and who you are *without* the fig leaves? Are you afraid to be left alone in silence with your own thoughts? Because in the nakedness, there is exposure; in the nakedness, there is flesh.

When you peel back the titles, maybe you have to face the fact that you have an anger problem. When you wipe off the makeup, maybe you have to face the fact that you have some insecurities. That's okay. I'm not here to make you feel even worse about yourself. I am simply here to remind you that you don't need permission to be human because it is inevitable. What I'm here to tell you is that in your weakness, God is strong.

As I mentioned earlier, I spent most of my twenties people-pleasing and then got to a point where I felt weak and almost at my wit's end. I remember writing a long letter to God on my thirtieth birthday, pouring my heart out to Him, talking about the hurt, the feeling of being overwhelmed, the discouragement, the pain—all of it. Sometimes we need those moments in our walk with Christ where we can be completely raw and real. These moments truly help to unveil our most authentic self. At the very end of the letter, I made this woeful yet affirming cry to God:

"I don't want to be a leader or a follower, I just want to be God's daughter."

You see, I was tired of the positions, I was tired of the labels, and I was tired of comparing myself and my portion to others. I knew that the place I felt most purely myself, loved and cherished, was in my rightful position as a daughter of God. That moment right there changed everything and set a new trajectory and path for me as I transitioned into a new decade and my thirties. I am not the same woman I was twenty years ago, when I thought that the key to success was achieving greater levels of status, opportunities, and connections. I am a woman who is thriving in my purpose while content in my role as *just* a daughter. The moment I realized this was the moment the conception of this book, *The Beauty of Being*, took place.

When you shed all the layers, you will find that you are *just a daughter*, and you are *just enough*.

You may be thinking, "Hold up! Are you trying to belittle me and minimize my worth?" Far from it. The word *just* can sometimes carry a negative connotation, depending on the way it is used. Many of us are even guilty of using this word as a weapon against ourselves in the name of false humility. For example, maybe you have used the word *just* in a way that diminishes your value and said phrases such as, "I'm just a stay-at-home mom" or "I'm just a beginner." Being a stay-at-home mom is one of the greatest and most impactful jobs on the earth and being a beginner at something makes you brave and willing to learn. Being *just a daughter* is not about what you aren't, but it's about all you *are*. One of my purposes for writing this book is to shift your perspective of identity from one that is fragmented and missing pieces to one that is whole and secure.

This world is temporary, and every title, every position, and every stage of life you attain will eventually expire. That is why your foundation should always be the Lord. In a world that is ever changing, He is the one constant where you can remain rooted, not to simply survive but to thrive. Be confident of this: your title and position as God's daughter can never be taken away from you; it is eternal. Moreover, nothing in this world, above it or below it, can ever separate you from the love that God has for you. (See Romans 8:39.) As a daughter of God, the Father's love for you is unconditional. You can find rest and true security in knowing that His love does not change depending on your work or good performance. It is here to stay. Just like my daughter does not stop being my daughter when she falls short of my expectations, you don't stop being God's daughter when you happen to miss the mark.

YOU ARE JUSTIFIED

Did you know that the reason why you are *just* enough as a daughter is because your identity as God's daughter was *justified* in heaven's court? *Justice* was served on the enemy when you were ransomed by Christ's blood shed for you on the cross.

The word *just* in Greek has several interesting and powerful meanings. *Just* is the root of the word *justice*. It also means "simply" and "righteous." When I say *just a daughter*, I am saying that being God's daughter is *simple*. You don't have to complicate it, add to it, or work for it. You just have to take your rightful position by accepting Jesus Christ as the Lord and Savior of your life. What is your rightful position? Your rightful position is righteous. Remember, the word "righteous" is one of the Greek translations for the word *just*. To be righteous is to be in right standing with God. To be righteous is to be seated with Christ in heavenly places. That is your position as *just a daughter*, and it is greater than any other position or title that you will ever have in this world.

When Jesus walked this earth nearly two thousand years ago, He came against the legalism perpetrated by the Pharisees. With Christ's death, burial, and resurrection, He set a new precedent for us to live by. At the moment that Christ gave His last breath, the veil of the temple was torn. (See Matthew 27:51.) The piece of fabric that once separated God from ma n, that only the high priests could go beyond into the holy of holies of God's presence, was no longer relevant. Now, Jews and gentiles alike, covered under the blood of Jesus, are encouraged to enter boldly into the throne of grace. (Hebrews 4:16)

> *But whenever someone turns to the Lord, the veil is taken away. For the Lord is the Spirit, and wherever the Spirit of the Lord is, there is freedom. So all of us who have had that veil removed can see and reflect the glory of the Lord. And the Lord—who is the Spirit—makes us more and more like him as we are changed into his glorious image.*
>
> (2 Corinthians 3:16–18 NLT)

Here's what we can take away from this Scripture:

+ Living for the Lord comes with the removal of the veil. This could also mean the removing of fig leaves or the idolatry of labels, status, position, and masks.

+ When you are no longer in bondage to people or the pressures of this world, you begin to walk in the Spirit and experience true freedom.

+ The beauty of being takes place when people can see the reflection of God's glory over their lives.

+ We become better followers of God when we humble ourselves and solely model our lives after Christ, rather than comparing ourselves to idols.

The removal of the veil, in essence, represents the undoing of humanity's fig leaves. *The fig leaves were first worn when sin was born. Then the veil was finally torn when our sin, through Christ, was borne.* Christ bore our sins, carried our sins, and triumphed over death, hell, and the grave. He reversed the curse, and now, because of Jesus's sacrifice, we don't just know God religiously; we have the honor of knowing Him relationally.

> *For the sin of this one man, Adam, caused death to rule over many. But even greater is God's wonderful grace and his gift of righteousness, for all who receive it will live in triumph over*

sin and death through this one man, Jesus Christ.

(Romans 5:17 NLT)

We no longer need the fig leaves; we no longer need the temple veil. We no longer need the layers that we put on in an attempt to hide from God and be accepted by man. That is why Isaiah the prophet says, *"All our righteous acts are like filthy rags"* (Isaiah 64:6). We can't take any confidence in our works in an attempt to achieve righteousness, yet we can take full confidence in God's work in and through us, even despite the process.

Daughter, what filthy rags have been separating you from the greater place of intimacy with the Father that you desire? What veils have you created in your life that need to be torn? True intimacy, in any form, requires a degree of nakedness and vulnerability. If you want to grow in intimacy with the Father, you can't be ashamed of your frailty and fragility. The Bible says we can enter the throne of grace with boldness.

THE DAUGHTER IN LUKE 8

I want to share the story of a woman who had filthy rags of her own. She was someone overlooked, unseen, but she knew that if she could align herself with Jesus and just be close enough to touch Him, she would be healed. This woman had been *"bleeding for twelve years, but no one could heal her"* (Luke 8:43). Just like her, many of us have spent years walking around with filthy rags, fig leaves, and labels that have been placed on us by others or sometimes even ourselves. We have tried to use these things as bandages to patch up our brokenness. We've sought wholeness and fulfillment in all the wrong places, when all we've truly needed is to be healed and made whole by the Father.

The woman with the issue of blood was among a multitude when she proceeded to touch the hem of Christ's garment. Out of what seemed to be a sea of people, she immediately stood out to

Christ when He felt the power go from Him by her touch. Like me and you, this woman had filthy rags that needed washing—and I'm not just talking about in the natural, but spiritually as well. Just imagine how discouraging it must have been to be bleeding nonstop for twelve years without a cure. Imagine going from physician to physician, hoping for a breakthrough, only to come up empty time after time. I can imagine how desperate she was for Jesus to change her situation and make her whole.

Then finally, after one encounter with Jesus, her life changed. Though still hidden among the multitude, she was still noticed and sought after by Jesus.

> *But Jesus said, "Somebody touched Me, for I perceived power going out from Me." Now when the woman saw that she was not hidden, she came trembling; and falling down before Him, she declared to Him in the presence of all the people the reason she had touched Him and how she was healed immediately.*
>
> (Luke 8:46–47 NKJV)

What's interesting is that from this Scripture, we see that the woman was used to being hidden and unseen. She did not expect Christ to notice her among the crowd, but she trembled in humility, reverence, and worship.

I need you to understand the distinction of your relationship with God as a daughter. The dynamic of this relationship is not like any other type of relationship. It is not even like the relationship between a father and son. The relationship between a father and a daughter is very unique and precious in nature.

Several times in the Bible, Jesus refers to women as "daughters," expressing His gentle and caring love for women. This is significant too especially in a time when women were seen as property, in a world where women are often objectified. God wants us to see women relationally as He sees them, as precious daughters worthy of love, care, and protection.

Jesus told the woman with the issue of blood, *"Daughter, your faith has healed you. Go in peace and be freed from your suffering"* (Mark 5:34).

Naturally, the father is seen as the provider and covering of the daughter until she is married. If she has an interested suitor, that man must ask the father for the woman's hand in marriage, and it is the father who is traditionally expected to walk the daughter down the aisle and hand her over in marriage. The daughter is dependent on the father in a way that makes her hidden. Her wedding is one of the rare times when we see a veil that is pure and warranted. It is the veil that the bride uses to cover her face as a sign of her protection, hiddenness, and being set apart until marriage. Then, when she meets her groom at the altar, the veil is removed. It is a reflection of Christ and the church; when He died for us and saved us, the veil was also removed from the world. It is a great mystery of deep significance, but these details are not trivial or random in nature. They are intentional.

HIDDEN IN GOD

A daughter is one who is hidden in God, for she is extremely valuable. Think about your most prized possessions. Are they hidden and protected? Or are they vulnerable and exposed? When you are hidden in Christ, you may feel overlooked by other people, but don't worry, the Father knows exactly where you are at all times. You are precious to Him.

For you died, and your life is hidden with Christ in God.
(Colossians 3:3)

I want us to dive further into this concept of being hidden because I recognize that it's often our insecurities in this area and our desire to be seen that usually lead us to search for fulfillment and affirmation from sources outside of Christ.

We seek labels to be seen. We perform to be seen. We desire to be recognized and appreciated because it makes us feel valued. But one of the greatest revelations I've had is that our value does not come from these things. You can be valued even when you're hidden. If you feel hidden in this season of life right now, it's probably because God values you and is protecting you.

I remember going through a season where I was single and wanted to be in a relationship. I wanted to be married; I wanted the labels of wife and mom. But it seems that in that season, nobody was checking for me, as if the guys were interested in everyone else but me. At the time, it felt like rejection was trying to pull away at my sense of worth until I came to realize that man's rejection sometimes is truly God's protection. There is a time for everything, and at that time, it was too early for me to awaken love. The Bible says, *"I charge you, O daughters of Jerusalem, do not stir up nor awaken love until it pleases"* (Song of Solomon 8:4 NKJV). In other words, daughter of God, do not rush whatever season or moment you are in, even if you feel hidden. Know that you are still valued, right where you are. At the right time, God revealed me and I found my husband. Now we've been married for twelve years and I find that God is faithful to fulfill His promises, but it must be in His perfect timing.

I want to give you one more example of a time when I felt hidden and overlooked, but I was in a season of observing, learning, and serving. For years, God had me faithfully and humbly serving another ministry before He called me to step out and start my own. He taught me so much during that time—what to do, what not to do, how to treat people, how to be professional, how to plan ministry events, and how to operate in the anointing. I learned so much, from practical to spiritual, but I have to admit that during this great season of immense growth, I faced some challenges that made me wonder if I would ever be ready to fulfill God's own personal plan and calling on my life. I had helped people accomplish their goals and build their visions without truly being appreciated for my contributions. I've had people steal my God-given creative ideas, and I've even given many of them up willingly. I've served the vision of others faithfully, many times never even seeking financial compensation or monetary gain because I knew that God just called me to serve without expecting anything in return from the people I was serving.

Yet I knew that one day, God would have me step out and do ministry on my own. But it wasn't until years later that He actually did release me to do it. I had to know who I was before it was time to walk in my calling. God had been revealing my spiritual gifts to me and the burden on my heart for the lost before He even began training me in ministry. I was born with a purpose.

WALKING WITH PURPOSE

People have this misconception that if you're not actively "walking in your purpose," you have a spiritual deficit. But you could be walking *with* purpose before you actually walk *in* your purpose. You carry that gifting, you have the anointing, but you just don't know it yet.

I love the story of David, who was a shepherd before he carried the title and role of a king. While he was shepherding the sheep, others may have judged him and assumed that his purpose was not so great. Even David's own father, Jesse, didn't think enough of his youngest son to present him to Samuel when the prophet was sent to anoint a new king for Israel. (See 1 Samuel 16:10–11.) Yet no one had any idea that something was brewing on the inside of David. God was preparing him to carry out the call on his life. David was walking with purpose before he was technically walking *in* his purpose. This is evident when he tells King Saul, *"Your servant has killed both the lion and the bear; this uncircumcised*

Philistine will be like one of them, because he has defied the armies of the living God" (1 Samuel 17:36). David was already a warrior before he battled Goliath, which is the event that worked as a catalyst to put him on the map. Before that, David was hidden in the pastures and fields, tending to the sheep. Although man didn't see David for who he was, God saw him. When Samuel went to the house of Jesse to anoint the next king, he made assumptions about David's brothers, who looked fit to rule and seemed worthy of the anointing.

> But the LORD said to Samuel, "Do not consider his appearance or his height, for I have rejected him. The LORD does not look at the things people look at. People look at the outward appearance, but the LORD looks at the heart."
>
> (1 Samuel 16:7)

God didn't want the obvious. God didn't want the ones who were recognized and in the spotlight for all to see. God wanted David, the one who was hidden, because He saw David's heart and He watched how David took care of the sheep even when no one was looking. He chose David, not his older brothers.

> Jesse had seven of his sons pass before Samuel, but Samuel said to him, "The LORD has not chosen these." So he asked Jesse, "Are these all the sons you have?" "There is still the youngest," Jesse answered. "He is tending the sheep." Samuel said, "Send for him; we will not sit down until he arrives."
>
> (1 Samuel 16:10–11)

I just want to encourage you that when you feel hidden and overlooked, stay faithful in serving God right where you are. You don't have to chase titles, acclaim, recognition, or status. When you truly serve God and live for Him, blessings look for you and find you. Goodness and mercy follow you. (See Psalm 23:6 NKJV.)

At the right time, they sent for David, and at the right time, God will send for you. Even after David was anointed, he didn't get on the throne and become king right away. He had to go through the same process that we talked about in chapter 1. David had to be prepared, perfected, purified, and proofed.

FEARFULLY AND WONDERFULLY MADE

My question to you is, even without the labels, are you truly confident in your position as a daughter of the King? If yes, proclaim the following truth with conviction:

> *I praise you because I am fearfully and wonderfully made;*
> *your works are wonderful, I know that full well.*
>
> (Psalm 139:14)

Yes, you may be imperfect. Yes, you may fall short sometimes. But do you believe that despite all that, you are a daughter of God who is fearfully and wonderfully made? Do you accept the fact that both of these truths can coexist? You can be flawed and human yet still beautifully precious to God, all at the same time. One does not negate the other. God does not love you less when you *do less*. We must shift our focus off of ourselves and our own works and shift our focus on to God with an attitude of praise as David does in Psalm 139.

> *Great and marvelous are Your works, Lord God Almighty!*
> *Just and true are Your ways, O King of the saints!*
>
> (Revelation 15:3 NKJV)

3

THE DOCTRINE OF "DOING"

Many of us have grown so accustomed to *doing* that somewhere along the line, we started to associate our identity, value, and worth with what we do. Yet this is a slippery slope to trek. What we *do* can change in an instant. Even our ability to *do* can be taken away from us if not for the grace of God. God forbid we are laid off from that job tomorrow, or we can't perform a skill the way we used to. During this life and walk of faith, we must learn the distinction between temporal and eternal. *Doing* is temporary because it is based on an act. *Being* is eternal because it is based on a fact. You are not what you do because your acts are temporary. But you can be who God says you are because His Word is eternal.

When God spoke you into existence, your identity became a fact. As daughters of God, we no longer have to prove our worth, but we can rest in the blessed assurance of God's Word. The beauty of God's omnipotent and omnipresent nature is that He is steadfast and a stronghold for those who take refuge in Him. You can find peace in knowing God is immovable, faithful, and true.

This helps us to rely more on God and what He can do and less on our own abilities. Scripture tell us many times, in several ways, that we cannot inherently do anything on our own but only through God alone.

John 15:5 (NLT) says, *"Yes, I am the vine; you are the branches. Those who remain in me, and I in them, will produce much fruit. **For apart from me you can do nothing.**"*

Another familiar verse says, *"**I can do all things through Christ** who strengthens me"* (Philippians 4:13 NKJV).

Scripture makes it very clear that anything we accomplish in this life, or anything that we do well, is done only because God allows us the strength and grace to do it. If that is the case, why is there so much false teaching coming from the false doctrine that I call *the doctrine of doing?* Unfortunately, I once subscribed to this works-based doctrine, which is heavily reliant on self and motivated by fear when we should always be reliant on God and motivated by faith. It is a doctrine that heavily promotes obedience, which is important, but it falls short by neglecting the importance of the fruit of the Spirit—*"love, joy, peace, patience, kindness, goodness, faithfulness, gentleness, and self-control"* (Galatians 5:22–23 NLT). This fruit is what enables us to be obedient in the first place.

LIVING IN THE FLESH

If you constantly hear preaching about "doing what God has called you to do" and "being obedient to God" but the fruit of the Spirit and character of God are never preached or lived out, then you've heard the doctrine of doing. None of us are capable of doing the things we should without the empowerment of the Holy Spirit because *"the spirit is willing, but the flesh is weak"* (Matthew 26:41). You cannot "do what God has called you to do" or "be obedient" when you are living in the flesh, when you are nasty, mean, gossiping, filled with lust, always arguing, or angry. The Pharisees operated from a religious spirit; following the doctrine of doing, they kept all the laws but had no fruit of the Spirit to really live a life that was pleasing to God.

The apostle Paul says:

> *I do not understand what I do. For what I want to do I do not do, but what I hate I do. And if I do what I do not want to do, I agree that the law is good. As it is, it is no longer myself who do it, but it is sin living in me. For I know that good itself does not dwell in me, that is, in my sinful nature. For I have the desire to do what is good, but I cannot carry it out. For I do not do the good I want to do, but the evil I do not want to do—this I keep on doing. Now if I do what I do not want to do, it is no longer I who do it, but it is sin living in me that does it.* (Romans 7:15–20)

We have all fallen short of the glory of God and our righteousness only comes by grace through faith in Christ Jesus. None of us can boast. None of us should be relying on our own strength, but we should all humble ourselves and recognize our need for the Savior, Jesus Christ.

As I said before, for many years, I lived by the dangerous doctrine of doing. Now let me explain. For a decade of my life, most of the messages and sermons I listened to were about "doing what God has called you to do," "stepping out in faith," and "acting in obedience." Now these messages are great when integrated within sound doctrine and a balanced presentation of Scripture. Yet when these messages are rooted in fear-mongering tactics and control, they can be detrimental to the body of Christ. I was under the impression that if I did not always *do* something, I was a purposeless Christian. If I was not being extreme and taking a huge *leap of faith*, then I was not pleasing God.

FAITH IS NOT MEANT TO BE A LEAP

But when did we begin assuming faith always had to be a leap? Why are we so quick to use the world's lingo, "leap of faith," which unfortunately encourages extremism, when God in His Word uses the example of faith as that of a mustard seed.

> *So Jesus said to them, "Because of your unbelief; for assuredly, I say to you, if you have faith as a mustard seed, you will say to this mountain, 'Move from here to there,' and it will move; and nothing will be impossible for you."*
>
> (Matthew 17:20 NKJV)

Nowhere does the Bible use the phrase "leap of faith." This false doctrine unfortunately has people rushing into things prematurely, resulting in unnecessary loss, pain, suffering, and spiritual warfare. You are out of order if you are taking leaps without pausing to labor in prayer and follow the leading of the Holy Spirit. This faith journey is not a leap or a sprint; it's a walk. The Bible says in 2 Corinthians 5:7 (NKJV), *"For we walk by faith, not by sight,"* and in Hebrews 11:1 (NKJV), *"Now faith is the substance of things hoped for, the evidence of things not seen."*

So imagine leaping or sprinting in the dark with a blindfold on. You would trip, fall, and get hurt. It is the same in the spirit realm as it is in the natural realm. When you can see but don't know where you are going, the most effective way to navigate the journey is walking, step by step. Now imagine yourself again in the dark with a blindfold on, but this time, you are still, standing in place and waiting on the Lord for the next instruction. You cannot see, you are in the dark, but you have the light of the Lord inside of you and you have the leading of the Holy Spirit to guide you.

He whispers and says, "Take two steps left." You, with your little mustard seed of faith, are obedient to that first instruction, and you take two steps left. Then He says, "Take one step forward." With your mustard seed of faith, you take one step forward. This is a daily walk of stepping in obedience to the Lord.

Stop taking crazy leaps and making unwise decisions that you'll regret and have to pay the consequences for in the future. Are you being still in the presence of the Lord today? Are you allowing the peace of the Holy Spirit to be your guide?

However, when He, the Spirit of truth, has come, He will guide you into all truth; for He will not speak on His own authority, but whatever He hears He will speak; and He will tell you things to come. (John 16:13 NKJV)

FAITH THE SIZE OF A MUSTARD SEED

God said that with faith the size of a mustard seed, we can move mountains. The beauty of a mustard seed is that it is so small, yet it yields such great and lasting results over time.

Jesus says:

To what shall we liken the kingdom of God? Or with what parable shall we picture it? It is like a mustard seed which, when it is sown on the ground, is smaller than all the seeds on earth; but when it is sown, it grows up and becomes greater than all herbs, and shoots out large branches, so that the birds of the air may nest under its shade. (Mark 4:30–32 NKJV)

Your faith may feel a little bit like a mustard seed. You may be comparing it to others who seem to be more radical in their faith. Maybe they quit their job to start a new business or maybe they just moved to a new country. You may think, "Man, they have huge faith," but please don't despise small beginnings. God will build up your faith little by little, day by day, as you stay in step with Him. One day, your faith will resemble the size of a ten- to fifteen-foot-tall mustard plant and just as wide. But remember, even with faith the size of a mustard seed, you can still make mountains move.

Your mustard seed of faith needs to be planted, rooted, and watered in order to grow. It needs time to germinate and soak in all the nutrients from the soil. Germination is the process in which a seed sprouts. Four things are required for a seed to germinate:

+ Water

+ Oxygen

+ Light

+ Warmth

It is the same for a spiritual seed of faith that is planted. We need to be rooted and washed with the cleansing of God's Word (see Ephesians 5:26); we need the *ruach* wind or breath of God[4] to speak and breathe on our seed, just as He did to form Adam from the ground (see Genesis 2:7); and our seed needs the warmth of sunlight, Jesus, *"the light of the world"* (John 8:12) and *"the true vine"* (John 15:1) from which we can grow. He is *"the way and the truth and the life"* (John 14:6).

If we want our faith to grow into great big trees and bear much fruit, we must keep the light of Christ in our lives. Being in Him is our foundation, for apart from Him, we can *"do nothing"* (John 15:5). God is first concerned with you being in Him before He is concerned with anything that you do. That is why the doctrine of *doing* is so dangerous and I wrote this book to emphasize the beauty of simply *being*. God desires for us to remain in Him.

Jesus says, *"I am the vine; you are the branches. If you remain in me and I in you, you will bear much fruit"* (John 15:5). The apostle

---

4. H7308. ruach. *Strong's Hebrew Concordance.*

Paul explains, *"For in him we live and move and have our **being**"* (Acts 17:28).

As a former pageant queen, I used to compete for titles. Sometimes I would win or place among the finalists; other times, I would walk away empty-handed. I want to share about a time when I lost a pageant but left that situation discovering more of who I really am instead of who I thought I wanted to be. I spent thousands of dollars and sacrificed hundreds of hours preparing for just a few minutes on that stage. I competed for a chance to win a fleeting crown that I would eventually have to pass on to a successor after my year of reign was over.

After laying it all on the line for a temporary title, I stood there, with sore feet and a tired smile, hoping and praying that they would call my name to be in the top fifteen. Name after name was announced, and little by little, my dream faded away like smoke from the fog machine and faint cheers of the audience that fizzled out in the distance.

It was as if time froze before my eyes, and God was teaching me something in that very moment. While I was hoping and praying for my name to be recognized and called out by man, I was reminded that I already serve a God who has called me by name.

But now, thus says the LORD, who created you, O Jacob, and He who formed you, O Israel: "Fear not, for I have redeemed you; I have called you by your name; You are Mine."

(Isaiah 43:1 NKJV)

WHAT COUNTS IS BEING CHOSEN BY GOD

Though I did not win an earthly crown that night, nor was I picked as a top fifteen finalist, I am still *chosen* by God. My hope is to one day receive the crown of life, when I meet my Maker and true Judge at the door of eternity.

I spent the pageant weekend being judged and scored by man. I was rated on my performance and presentation on stage. I was compared to other women based on my stature, body, and physique. As a mom of four, I felt confident about my body, but in the eyes of man, it could not compete against the abs, toned legs, and sculpted figures that many of the other contestants were able to obtain.

I am so glad that I serve a God who does not simply judge me by my appearance, performance, or presentation. I am so glad that I serve a God who sees the heart. He saw David's heart and chose him to be anointed as king. (See 1 Samuel 16:7, 12–13.)

Just as David was overlooked when it came to the lineup of his brothers, I too felt this way. During this certain pageant, though I was one of the shorter contestants, I was always placed in the back, while those of higher stature were highlighted in the front. My family, who was in the audience, even mentioned that they could hardly see me during the show.

Regardless, I thank God that He can still see me through all the smoke, blinding lights, confetti, and noise. The judges may have missed the most beautiful parts of me that weekend, but God saw everything. I wasn't the loudest. I wasn't the most prominent, the most flashy, or even the most attractive. Yet true beauty is not defined by those temporary things anyway.

First Peter 3:3–4 says, "*Your beauty should not come from outward adornment, such as elaborate hairstyles and the wearing of gold jewelry or fine clothes. Rather, it should be that of your inner self, the unfading beauty of a gentle and quiet spirit, which is of great worth in God's sight.*"

The *beauty of being* has more to do with the quiet and gentle spirit than it has to do with your outward appearance. How do you cultivate this inward form of unfading beauty? It is done by implementing a spiritual beauty regimen that fashions your spirit man with the fruit we know to be the fruit of the Spirit: *"Love, joy, peace, patience, kindness, goodness, faithfulness, gentleness, and self-control* (Galatians 5:22–23 NLT).

These fruits are qualities of inner beauty that reflect the spirit of a true daughter of the King. The truth is many of these qualities directly contradict the world's standard of beauty.

For instance:

+ The Spirit exudes gentleness, but the world tells us to be fierce.

+ The Spirit produces self-control, but the world tells us we need sex appeal.

+ The Spirit brings goodness, but the world tells us that being *bad* is a compliment.

So what does a spiritual beauty regimen look like and how do you create one?

A SPIRITUAL BEAUTY REGIMEN

A spiritual beauty regimen accentuates the fruit of the Spirit and gives us that godly glow from the inside out. To further answer this question, we can observe the life of a beauty queen who radiated all these inner qualities and more. The beauty queen I am referring to is Queen Esther from the Bible. Esther was actually in a beauty pageant as well. Though she was beautiful on the outside, what made her stand out in the eyes of the king was the favor of God in her life. I took time to study the favor of God, especially in the context of Esther's situation, and I want to go a little deeper into how one can obtain this type of favor.

We've all heard the saying, "Beauty is in the eye of the beholder." But favor is a gateway from God in which He has opened someone's eyes to behold you to begin with.

So how did God favor Esther in such a way that the king's eyes were opened and keen to behold her as queen from among all the other concubines? (See Esther 2:17.) Esther stood out; she was highlighted and had a special glow about her. She had a spiritual beauty regimen that caused her to shine. The very face of God beamed off of Esther as she embodied His peace in all her interactions with the king. He was drawn to Esther, who seemed to have possessed the favor of God and blessing spoken of in Numbers 6:24–26:

> The LORD bless you and keep you; the LORD make his face shine on you and be gracious to you; the LORD turn his face toward you and give you peace.

Imagine spending so much time in the Lord's presence that His very face begins to shine upon you and radiate off of you wherever you go. What type of spiritual beauty regimen would produce this level of glow-up? Well, it's no secret. There are several beauty treatments that you can incorporate into a spiritual beauty regimen for the ultimate glow-up from the inside out:

THE PROCESS OF PATIENCE

Patience is an essential process when it comes to natural beauty. For instance, taking care of your skin, hair, and nails all take a level of patience to bring about some good results. In the same way, when it comes to our spiritual journey of beautification, God is making us beautiful through the process of patience.

Scripture says, *"But let patience have its perfect work, that you may be perfect and complete, lacking nothing"* (James 1:4 NKJV).

When we lack patience spiritually, we can tend to lash out of the flesh and things can quickly get ugly. Impatient people are more likely to express feelings of anger, frustration, or hatred. Impatience can even cause stress and anxiety, which takes away from the beautifying qualities of peace and calm. No one is attracted to someone who is always complaining, on edge, or in a rush. No, if you want people to see the light in you, growing in patience is a great way to start.

THE FOOD OF FASTING

I've witnessed firsthand fasting truly has the ability to give you a special glow. Seriously, when you fast the right way, your countenance begins to change because you are spending so much time in God's presence. This is what happened to Moses after he spent forty days and forty nights fasting and in the Lord's presence on Mount Sinai.

> Now it was so, when Moses came down from Mount Sinai (and the two tablets of the Testimony were in Moses' hand when he came down from the mountain), that Moses did not know that the skin of his face shone while he talked with Him.
>
> (Exodus 34:29 NKJV)

After a time of fasting and praying, I feel spiritually energized and renewed, sometimes even more youthful. People may use anti-aging beauty products for a more youthful and vibrant look, but that can be spiritually achieved through fasting and prayer. Also, after feasting on God's Word and removing processed foods and drinks from your diet, you may experience a natural clearing effect on your skin.

SABBATH REST AND RELAXATION

Beauty sleep is known to work when it comes to natural beauty, but did you know that this is effective when it comes to spiritual beauty as well? When you stress less, trust God more, embrace peace, and get rid of all that stress and anxiety, your entire essence changes. You are more calm, the Spirit of God begins to shine through, and you have a completely different aura about you.

In the midst of a world that is hustling nonstop, wreaking havoc and chaos, you can have peace and rest in the Lord. That is our inheritance, that is our blessing as children of God—we should have peace and rest for God has *"overcome the world"* (John 16:33). When we walk in the blessing of God's peace, God's face shines upon us, giving us a godly, glowing countenance.

SPIRITUAL ANOINTING AND CONSECRATION

Now let's talk about spiritual anointing and consecration. Naturally, oils are used for beautification purposes because they bring moisture, shine, and glow to the skin, hair, and nails. Sometimes oils are also scented and carry a nice, attractive smell. This is why oil was used to prepare all the king's concubines with their beauty treatments regimen in the book of Esther.

But spiritually, oil plays a significant role as well. It represents the power and presence of the Holy Spirit. It is also used to represent one who stands out and has the anointing, one with God's favor and blessing. In the natural, a beautiful person is one who would stand out in a room; people notice that there is something different and special about that person. It is the same way with the oil of God and anointing of God in the spirit. It will set you apart and cause you to stand out because you have the anointing. David, who was anointed by the prophet Samuel to be king, was handsome on the outside as well as the inside.

So Jesse sent for him. He was dark and handsome, with beautiful eyes. And the LORD said, "This is the one; anoint him."
(1 Samuel 16:12 NLT)

I personally like to anoint my own children and anoint myself often, before bed and also before performing any type of ministry activity. I know that God has called me *"for such a time as this"* (Esther 4:14) and set me apart to do His will.

THE PERFUME OF PRAYER

The last spiritual beauty treatment that I would like to mention is the perfume of prayer. Believe it or not, if you smell good, you look even better, despite what you've been through. No one can tell what you've been through when you spray yourself with a nice perfume, and in the same way, people are not able to tell what you've been through when you get on your face and pray, releasing your cares and worries to God. Yet despite the ugly and stinky circumstances you may have walked through in life, your prayer always releases a beautifully scented aroma to the Father.

As one of David's psalms says, *"Let my prayer be set before You as incense, the lifting up of my hands as the evening sacrifice"* (Psalm 141:2 NKJV).

4

"LIKE A CHILD"

*Then people brought little children to Jesus for him to place
his hands on them and pray for them. But the disciples
rebuked them. Jesus said, "Let the little children come to me,
and do not hinder them,
for the kingdom of heaven belongs to such as these."*
—Matthew 19:13–14

In chapter 1, we briefly touched on the idea of returning to a state
of spiritual infancy, where you become more reliant on God and
shift from restless to rested. It is through this experience that your
childlike faith is reignited and your identity as a daughter of God
is reclaimed. You are made bare before the Lord, just as a babe
enters into the world in its nakedness and fragility. The burdens
and cares of this life that you are carrying are now surrendered to
the Lord, for He is now your primary caretaker.

Give all your worries and cares to God, for he cares about
you.　　　　　　　　　　　　　　　　(1 Peter 5:7 NLT)

You may say, "But Karolyne, I don't have time to rest; I work full time," or "I don't have time to read my Bible. I can barely get a moment to myself." Listen, I hear you and I understand your frustration. At different points in my life, I made those excuses too. I was always super busy, I didn't believe in honoring the sabbath, I failed to be consistent in my devotional time, and so on. But staying there would have gotten me nowhere. I would not be able to grow spiritually in my walk with Christ, and I would not have the ability to experience the fullness of being as He desires me to. So I had to make a change.

RETURNING TO A CHILDLIKE FAITH

Here are the specific steps that I would recommend taking if you want to boost your level of childlike faith and return to a posture of complete dependence on God. These are the tips that helped me embrace the beauty of being in my life while also watching God transform me spiritually as well as the lives of those around me.

KEEP TRACK OF YOUR PRAYER REQUESTS

One of the things I noticed that really helped increase my prayer life and restore my childlike faith in God was keeping track of my prayer life. I even created a fun and comfy space in my home that is dedicated to praying and spending time with God. Many children have a room or a space where they spend much of their time and save all their creations and things that they are working on. As children of God, it's a good idea to set aside a place to pray and meet with God intimately, even if it's a closet or a tiny little corner or laundry room in your house. This idea isn't foreign or new; the Bible talks about this:

But when you pray, go into your room, close the door and pray to your Father, who is unseen. Then your Father, who sees what is done in secret, will reward you.   (Matthew 6:6)

But even more than just having a prayer room, I have started to track my prayers with a sense of expectation, which helps to build my faith. Just as a child makes a Christmas or birthday list for their parents to fulfill. Whenever my kids ask me something and I say I am going to do it, they never forget, trust me. And if I happen to forget something, they will be sure to remind me. They wait on me and trust that I will do what I have said. It's the same thing with God. He desires for us to believe He will accomplish what He has said.

In the past, I would pray casually here and there, without paying much attention to what I was praying or when I had prayed. Praying was very much just a routine habit for me because I thought, "That's what Christians are supposed to do, right?" For years, I prayed but I didn't actually believe that God listened to me or that He would answer. When He *did* answer my prayers, sometimes I wouldn't even notice or give Him thanks. I was not in a posture of expectation and hope; I was just religiously praying out of routine.

Then after God broke me free from operating under legalistic pretense, I had a renewed hope and faith in Him. I began writing my prayers down and actually paying close attention and keeping track of them. I found that God was often answering my prayers, close to 95 to 98 percent of the time, and I was actually shocked that my prayers were working. Now I pray all the time, even about the smallest things, and when God answers, it gets me excited and motivated to pray even more. My childlike faith is built up and encouraged in this way because I truly believe God sees me, hears me, loves me, and answers prayer. Prayer is powerful. I've seen God change the hearts of family members, fulfill creative desires, and meet natural, spiritual, and emotional means. He has done so much for me and others in so many ways, how can I not believe?

MODEL YOUR LIFE AFTER CHRIST

My next tip to achieve childlike faith is to model your life after Christ. Though this sounds cliché, this is something that we often forget to do. As someone who grew up wanting to be a fashion model, I am now able to spot the pitfalls associated with having idols as your muse rather than looking to Christ as your example. Kids naturally look up to people or model their lives after someone who is older than them because they want to learn and grow to become like that person. I have experienced this firsthand because my daughter copies a lot of what I do. She imitates the way I dress, the way I communicate, my favorite color, and the things I enjoy doing. One day, she was trying to walk around in my heels, and she told me that she wants to be just like her mama when she grows up.

Children are often encouraged to have a role model, then when those same children grow up to be adults, they are taught they need to *be* role models. They feel the need to be the person that others admire and look up to. They feel the pressure to have it all together or be the strong one in their group of friends. Though I would consider myself a role model to younger girls, I have to do a personal heart-check on occasion to make sure I remain humble because until we get to heaven, I don't think we'll ever *arrive*. It is from that place that we see many leaders fall.

Proverbs 16:18 says, *"Pride goes before destruction, a haughty spirit before a fall."*

Sadly, during my time as a Christian, I've experienced many leaders fall in the church due to pride. Pride is one of the most common entrapments that the enemy will use to pull someone away from God's purpose and calling for their life because they seek their own purpose and desires outside of God. That is what happened to Satan. Satan fell like lightning from heaven (see Luke

10:18) because pride had entered into his heart and he wanted to be like God. (See Isaiah 14:14.) Pride is a dangerous thing to play with. The Bible says, *"God opposes the proud but gives grace to the humble"* (James 4:6 NLT). I have personally watched someone that I once looked up to as a role model fall due to pride. It was sad to see them step outside of God's plan for their life and no longer operate in the same level of anointing they had before. God even led me to repent for allowing my admiration of this person to become idolatry in my life. Pride blinded me to the fact that this person was simply a human capable of making mistakes, as we all areand the only person we should truly model our life after is Jesus.

We are called to be ambassadors of Christ, for 2 Corinthians 5:20 (NKJV) says, *"Now then, we are ambassadors for Christ, as though God were pleading through us: we implore you on Christ's behalf, be reconciled to God."* An ambassador is an official representative of a country. As ambassadors of Christ, we represent the kingdom of God. The problem is, instead of being ambassadors for God's purposes and agenda, many of us, due to pride, become ambassadors for ourselves. This is the open door and loophole through which pride likes to enter. The idolatry of self and narcissism are calling cards for the spirit of pride. The Bible says that in the last days, *"People will be lovers of themselves, lovers of money, boastful, proud, abusive, disobedient to their parents, ungrateful, unholy"* (2 Timothy 3:2).

What do you love more, God or your idols? I'm harping on this a little because God has shown me just how deeply detrimental and serious idolatry is. It aims to rob God of His glory and hinders us from having the childlike faith that pleases God. Children are truly some of the most humble beings on earth. They know that they don't have all the answers. They are curious and seek after their parents. They know that they don't have the ability to care for themselves, so they go to their parents for daily provision, affection, and to meet their needs. We, as God's spiritual children, should do our best to return to this place of spiritual infancy and childlike faith if pride, self-sufficiency, and religious routines have pulled us away.

God is *"a jealous God"* (Exodus 20:5), and He will not tolerate any idol, not even the idol of self, to take His rightful place in your heart. We are called to die to self daily so that Christ may shine through us all the more. As His ambassadors, we understand:

> *I have been crucified with Christ; it is no longer I who live, but Christ lives in me; and the life which I now live in the flesh I live by faith in the Son of God, who loved me and gave Himself for me.* (Galatians 2:20 NKJV)

Jesus gave Himself for us and that is why we now live for Him. It is Christ who has given us a new identity, and we have become ambassadors for Christ, representatives of the kingdom of God. We have been sent out into the world as His disciples. You don't just wear the brand of heaven; you leave the imprint of heaven on earth wherever you go. In ancient times, a brand was not just a logo or an aesthetic, but a physical mark made with a hot iron used to denote ownership, servitude, or religious affiliation. God has not only marked you as one of His ambassadors; He has also commissioned you to leave a mark on this earth. This is the Great Commission, which says, *"Go therefore and make disciples of all the nations, baptizing them in the name of the Father and of the Son and of the Holy Spirit"* (Matthew 28:19 NKJV).

When you truly realize that your life is meant to be a reflection of one that is greater, an ode to the life of Christ, it humbles you. You receive a level of childlike faith when your sole admiration is for the Lord. As God's children, Jesus is the one who we should aspire to model our life after. To live like He lived and walk like He walked is the ultimate goal. A true disciple of Christ is not concerned with status. However, even while following Jesus, the disciples once wondered who would be the greatest in heaven.

> *At that time the disciples came to Jesus and asked, "Who, then, is the greatest in the kingdom of heaven?" He called a little child to him, and placed the child among them. And he said: "Truly I tell you, unless you change and become like little children, you will never enter the kingdom of heaven. Therefore, whoever takes the lowly position of this child is the greatest in the kingdom of heaven. And whoever welcomes one such child in my name welcomes me."* (Matthew 18:1–5)

As disciples of Christ, we are called to carry our cross and model our lives after Him. Though many may look up to us along the way, we should always remember that He is the ultimate role model and only person who anyone should follow.

APPLY YOUR FAITH THROUGH IMAGINATION

My third and final tip for increasing your childlike sense of faith is to apply your faith through imagination. Vision and creativity are such powerful, God-given tools and children tap into them from a very young age. Most children in school or even at Sunday school are often given arts and crafts to do and projects to paint, color, and draw. This is something that all children are encouraged to do and we really push young children to use their imaginations and be creative.

But when we reach adulthood, creativity and artistic expression are only encouraged for certain people thought to be creative or have a creative gifting. Yet I personally believe that all adults should be encouraged to continue practicing with some form of creative expression just as children are. We were all made in God's image, and God is the Creator of all things. If God is creative and we come from Him, I believe that we all have the ability to create in one way or another, but it may not be traditional or what others expect.

One person may be able to create great drawings or beautiful sculptures, while the other person's creative ability may be more logistical in nature, such as coming up with solutions to problems, or taking something small and turning it into something else, or making a delicious meal with a few ingredients, like my grandma would do. When I went on vacation with my grandma, we only had a few groceries available to use in the hotel room, but somehow she was able to make a feast out of nothing. That is *creative*. Jesus was a carpenter, but He performed many creative miracles, like the time He fed the multitude with just five loaves of bread and two fish. (See Matthew 14:16–21.)

I encourage you to be more self-aware of the opportunities that God gives you to express your creativity because He is inviting you to exercise childlike faith, to use your imagination and faith in Him to envision and produce something special. This will not only make walking with Christ more fun, but it will also be a great way to bond and partner with the Holy Spirit.

I remember one time when I wanted to make a candy cart for my daughter's *princess carnival* themed birthday party. Instead of dishing out hundreds of dollars to purchase a candy cart for a one-time event, I resolved in my heart that with the help of the Holy Spirit, I would use my creativity and imagination to build the candy cart on my own. After a few days of worship, creating, praying, patience, and partnering with the Holy Spirit, I had successfully made a candy cart out of boxes that were taped together, a roof made of Styrofoam and cardboard, and handles made of toilet paper rolls and wrapping paper rolls. I prettied the cart up using paint, pretty wrapping paper, and some shiny fringe paper. Let me tell you, though it was a little lopsided and the little wheels were bending at the bottom, you could not tell me anything about my candy cart! My daughters loved it and it was kid approved! I was so proud of my creation because I used my creativity and the help of the Holy Spirit to bring this vision to life, and I'm sure God was proud. It's the same with a child—they look at their little drawings and scribbles at a young age, and they are so proud of them. They give you those little scribbles, and as a parent, you are so proud too because it came from such a pure and imaginative place—so much so that you place it on the refrigerator to be on display. You are pleased with your child. In the same way, when we use our creativity and exercise our faith in God, though it may look like scribble scrabble to the world, it looks like a masterpiece and work of art to our Father God. Right now, I imagine Him framing our lives and placing it upon His own personal wall in heaven.

> For **we are God's masterpiece**. He has created us anew in Christ Jesus, so we can do the good things he planned for us long ago.   (Ephesians 2:10 NLT)

OTHER WAYS TO EXERCISE CHILDLIKE FAITH

1. Expressing creativity during Bible study through a journaling Bible or a coloring Bible for adults.

2. Practicing Scripture memorization with fun, beautiful Scripture cards or creating or purchasing wall art and canvases to decorate your home with Scripture.

3. Making music for the Lord. Write songs or raps. Or if you're not a writer, take a worship song and remix the words just a little bit to make it personal to you and your relationship with God. What is your version of the song? You can customize it and use your expression of worship to draw closer to the Father.

DISCIPLES MUST BE DISCIPLINED

We talked about what it means to be an ambassador for Christ. Let's talk a little more about discipleship because a disciple is actually a *disciplined one*. Discipline in necessary to be a disciple of Jesus Christ, but discipline also affirms us as children of God. As a child of God's, it's important to understand the Lord's discipline and how it plays a role in our spiritual walk.

My greatest weakness—a lack of discipline—is the one thing that has caused me to lose opportunities. It's also become my biggest blessing because it has rooted me in a deeper revelation of God's love for me. It has made Romans 8:28 (NKJV) a reality for me: *"And we know that all things work together for good to those who love God, to those who are the called according to His purpose."*

For much of my life, I lacked discipline. I grew up with a single mom who did everything she could to raise me and provide the best life for me and my sisters. To this day, she always tells me, "You were such a good kid; you were easy," and I can see why she would say that. I didn't have many problems growing up. I was pretty sheltered, quiet at times, had a few friends, and was a low-maintenance kid. I didn't require much.

Yet we have been conditioned to believe that only *bad* kids need discipline. And we assume that if you *act good* then you must already be disciplined. The truth is, I was a good actor on the outside, but on the inside, I was a hurricane. I struggled with lust, porn, and gluttony. I appeared to be such a good kid, but on the inside, I was a mess.

According to my family, my mom is the *cool mom*. She is very laid back, chill, down to earth, and nonjudgmental. I was afforded a healthy amount of freedom, trust, and space growing up, which helped to nurture my independence, confidence, and creative spirit. I had opportunities to cultivate my gifts and talents from an early age and become an entrepreneur from my adolescence. For that, I am truly thankful. But as I grew into adulthood, I started to realize that something was missing. I had a lot of potential, but my lack of discipline became very evident once I got to college. I would procrastinate and wait until the last minute to write my English papers (though I always aced them), I fumbled some scholarships due to immaturity, and I was far from punctual when it came to important meetings and events. I had no clue how to operate in excellence. It just seemed natural for me to cut corners and take the easy way out of things. I would drop the ball in so many different areas, doing things to get them *done* rather than doing them from a place of excellence, order, and integrity so that God could get the glory. This lack of discipline caused a lot of losses, strife, and unnecessary debt in my life, yet I thank God it didn't last for long.

God stepped in as a faithful Father and literally saved me through discipline. He used my husband, mentors, and older men and women in my life to teach me the basics of how to have good character, how to be professional, and how to run a God-honoring kingdom business. Then as I continued to mature and grow in my walk of faith and relationship with God, I started to walk more closely with the Holy Spirit as my counselor and teacher. He literally taught me everything I needed to know. He showed me how to be excellent in business, how to treat clients and customers well, how to cultivate my gifts, how to care for people tenderly in ministry, and how to take the honorable road and not just the easy way out. God taught me how to work as unto Him, not for money and not as onto man.

> *Work willingly at whatever you do, as though you were working for the Lord rather than for people. Remember that the Lord will give you an inheritance as your reward, and that the Master you are serving is Christ.* (Colossians 3:23–24 NLT)

That is the beauty of a father's discipline. My mom did the best she could as a single mom. The very essence of a mother is more inclined to nurture. Yet on the other hand, a father is more naturally inclined to discipline and instruct. That is the example that God sets for us in His Word. One way to know we are children of God is if the Father disciplines us.

I want to make one thing clear: God does not just discipline His *bad* kids or the Christians who are backsliding. We are all in the same boat here. What the world considers *good* isn't always godly. You can look good by man's standards but still head straight to hell. God disciplines *all* of us. No matter how perfect your church attendance is or how many Bible verses you have memorized, you can't opt out of this. There is certain level of character building, inner work, and development that can only take place through the Father's discipline.

> *And have you forgotten the encouraging words God spoke to you as his children? He said, "My child, don't make light of the LORD's discipline, and don't give up when he corrects you. For the LORD disciplines those he loves, and he punishes each one he accepts as his child." As you endure this divine discipline, remember that God is treating you as his own children. Who ever heard of a child who is never disciplined by its father? If God doesn't discipline you as he does all of his children, it means that you are illegitimate and are not really his children at all. Since we respected our earthly fathers who disciplined us, shouldn't we submit even more to the discipline of the Father of our spirits, and live forever? For our earthly fathers disciplined us for a few years, doing the best they knew how. But God's discipline is always good for us, so that we might share in his holiness. No discipline is enjoyable while it is happening—it's painful! But afterward there will be a peaceful harvest of right living for those who are trained in this way.* (Hebrews 12:5–11 NLT)

Because we live in a sinful world, circumstances don't always reflect God's originally intended design and desire for our lives. As a good Father, God also wants His best for us, but sometimes due to sin, we end up in circumstances that fail to deliver the fruitful results that would have been produced if things were done God's way.

Now in my relationship with my heavenly Father God, I no longer despise discipline. I am grateful for it because I know that He loves me. He shows me the truth of my ways when I'm out of order, and sometimes it's a hard pill to swallow, but I've learned to embrace it, accept it, and grow from it.

SPIRITUAL IMMATURITY VS. SPIRITUAL INFANCY

There was a stage in my walk with the Lord when I used to get mad at God all the time when I didn't get my way or things didn't go as I'd expected ... until I realized that was a sign of spiritual immaturity. It's also important to note that spiritual immaturity is different from the spiritual infancy that we've been talking about.

Spiritual immaturity is when you are resisting more of God, which hinders your growth in Him. You are still driven by self and the lust of the flesh. Instead of the meat of God's truth, you settle for the milk. (See 1 Corinthians 3:2.) You have *"itching ears"* (2 Timothy 4:3) and only like to listen to feel-good messages that feed the flesh rather than edify your spirit. Instead of pursuing spiritual growth and growing intimacy in your walk in the Lord, you settle for safe. You're just trying to get your foot into the door of heaven but are barely escaping the flames. (See 1 Corinthians 3:15.) You teeter-totter on the line of your faith and are tossed to and fro like the waves of the sea. Spiritual immaturity can lead to doublemindedness, when you are unstable in all your ways. (See James 1:8.)

A spiritual immature Christian can eventually become luke-warm because they refuse to grow, and the fire for God begins to fizzle out. God tells such believers, "*Since you are like luke-warm water, neither hot nor cold, I will spit you out of my mouth!*" (Revelation 3:16 NLT).

I know some adults who are immature and petty, and I know some children who are mature beyond their years. It is the same in the body of Christ. Being a member of your church for many years or growing up in the church does not equate with spiritual maturity. The Pharisees had many years of traditions under their belts and thought they were spiritually superior but they were spiritually immature. What distinguishes spiritual infancy from spiritual immaturity is the newness that comes with being like a child. A baby or a young child approaches life with wonder. They are able to constantly renew their minds, take a posture of humility, and be eager to learn something new and grow. While those who are spiritually immature resist God, spiritual infancy draws people to latch on to Christ and depend on Him as their very life source. Spiritual infancy means being "*made new in the attitude of* [our] *minds*" and putting on "*the new self, created to be like God in true righteousness and holiness*" (Ephesians 4:23–24).

Spiritual immaturity will cause you to reject the discipline of God. Spiritual infancy, on the other hand, will lead you to embrace it. From my experience with God disciplining me in my spiritual infancy, I've learned that God is a good Father who just wants the best for me. So I stopped throwing spiritual temper tantrums and just started to trust Him. When you don't get what you want and things don't go as planned, still praise God anyway, because He's working things out for your good and He is doing an even greater work inside you.

My greatest weakness, lack of discipline, has become my biggest blessing because God's discipline literally saved me. Did you know that God disciplines us to keep us safe? Discipline gives us boundaries and parameters to hinder us from stepping outside of God's safety net. It is in God's nature to protect us. Think of the ocean. If God didn't tell the waves where to stop on the shore, we would not be able to safely enjoy the beach. We would be afraid that we could get washed up at any moment. If God did not align the earth perfectly on its axis and give it the exact speed and motion it needs to orbit the sun, we would not enjoy night and day and may even burn or freeze to death.

GOD'S BOUNDARIES PRESERVE HIS GLORY

When God sets a boundary in place, it's for a good reason, and many times that reason is not only to keep you safe but to preserve His glory. God gets glory out of us being able to enjoy the beach. God gets glory out of us being able to enjoy night and day without harm. When it comes to the beauty of being, discipline designs a safe boundary for us to simply *be* without a worry or a care. Imagine going down a big water slide that was missing the proper rails. What was intended to be fun and free could very easily hurt someone. God gets the glory when we walk holding on to the purposeful guardrails of His design. God even gets glory out of the messes we make if we allow Him to turn what the enemy intended for our bad so He can use it for our good.

I'm so glad that God could take my mess so that I can share this message. Because of discipline, I learned self-control. When God delivered me over a decade ago from porn, lust, and gluttony, I was already free, but I had to walk in the Spirit in order to maintain that freedom. I had to cultivate the fruit of the Spirit, one of them being self-control. So I can say *no* to lust, *no* to the flesh, *no* to the cookie or cake, because I am making the decision to be disciplined.

I say then: Walk in the Spirit, and you shall not fulfill the lust of the flesh. … But the fruit of the Spirit is love, joy, peace, longsuffering, kindness, goodness, faithfulness, gentleness, self-control. Against such there is no law. And those who are

Christ's have crucified the flesh with its passions and desires.
(Galatians 5:16, 22–24 NKJV)

When we are being disciplined by God, it sometimes feels like we are being punished and crucified. But be encouraged, you are crucified *with Christ.*

I have been crucified with Christ and I no longer live, but Christ lives in me. The life I now live in the body, I live by faith in the Son of God, who loved me and gave himself for me.   (Galatians 2:20)

Jesus endured the Father's discipline of the cross for our safety, to save us. The crucifixion of Jesus Christ is proof that He is the Messiah because it legitimizes Him as God's Son according to Hebrews 12. Jesus was literally crushed, whipped, beaten, and bruised for us.

But he was pierced for our rebellion, crushed for our sins. He was beaten so we could be whole. He was whipped so we could be healed.   (Isaiah 53:5 NLT)

Now let me be clear, I do not condone child abuse or harm to children. Because Jesus took the whips for us, we don't have to endure them. God did not have to whip me to discipline me. He was very gentle yet stern. He daily teaches me, leads me, and corrects me. When I take a wrong step, He redirects me. That is what true Spirit-filled discipline looks like. When you allow God to lead you and discipline you as a child, He imparts His heart to you and shows you how to be with your children and discipline them too. Sometimes when I get frustrated with my own kids for being disobedient or not listening, I just see myself in them and I think, "Wow, how gracious has the Lord been to me." Then I offer and extend that same grace and patience to my children. When you have truly experienced the loving discipline of the heavenly Father, it changes the way you discipline or treat the people in your life.

Since the discipline of the heavenly Father has entered my life, it not only delivered me and improved my relationships with others, but it improved every single area of my life. I am more disciplined in my eating habits and am living a more healthy and whole lifestyle so I can have the mobility and stamina needed to better serve and glorify God with my life and body as *the temple of the Holy Spirit*" (1 Corinthians 6:19 NKJV). My money management practices and financial wisdom have increased as a result of discipline, and for God's glory, I've been able to build generational wealth to secure my own children's future and also invest in the kingdom of God for His glory. These are just practical examples of how discipline and the fruit of self-control can spread and positively improve many areas of your life for the glory of God.

MEMBERS OF GOD'S ARMY

There is something different about you when you have truly been shaped, molded, and brought up in the discipline of the Lord. It's similar to people who have had Army training. People who have been in the Army are cut from a cloth of discipline that is easily recognizable just by observing their demeanor and how they carry themselves. Did you know that we have an Army Dad? He is *the LORD of hosts*" (Psalm 46:7 NKJV), "God of the armies of heaven." Did you know that you are a member of the army of God? That is one of the reasons why God has to discipline us as His children. Still, it's important to note that even as we face various trials, tribulations, and tests on this earth, we fight from a place of victory because ultimately, the battle is not ours—*the battle is the LORD's*" (1 Samuel 17:47).

That means that God fights on your behalf. Your job is not to fight, but to stand on His Word and truth. *"He says, 'Be still, and know that I am God'"* (Psalm 46:10). That is the beauty of being.

God has taken full responsibility in doing, so that we can rest in being.

Many times, the children of Army parents grow up very disciplined with routines, schedules, and structure. In the same way, we are God's army children, and God will call us to live disciplined lives as disciples of Christ. There is beauty in having a routine or structure. I realized that I wasn't able to truly embrace the beauty of being until I started resting in rhythms designed to facilitate calm rather than chaos. I traded in the vain busyness for practicality, peace, and purpose. To be a busybody is to be out of order and lack discipline. To the world, you may appear productive because you're booked and busy, but God knows when you are out of divine alignment and have wandered outside the bounds of what He has truly called you to do.

> *We hear that there are some who walk among you in a disorderly manner, not working at all, but are busybodies.*
> (2 Thessalonians 3:11 NKJV)

A good parent will create purposeful routines, structure, and rhythms of rest for their children to thrive in. This can look like sleep training, nap time, bath time, morning routines, or bedtime routines. As a mother of four, I can attest firsthand that giving your children some sort of structure helps to build their sense of security and confidence. At times when I have strayed from my toddler's routine, for example, it affects her mood and can make her cranky. She is left trying to figure out and understand her day rather than resting in the rhythms designed for her.

God does the same for us; He gives us rhythms in this life—morning, afternoon, and night, seasons and Sabbath rest. He does not expect us to worry about our life or come up with a new idea for every day. He expects us to rest in the rhythms as He orders our every step. When we resist the rhythms and try to do our own thing, just like a child, chaos ensues and we become overwhelmed. That's when we are most irritable and eventually experience burnout.

Ask yourself, "Have I stepped outside of the rhythms and boundaries that God has designed for my safety and peace?" Allow the Holy Spirit to reveal the answer to you. Maybe you are skipping a weekly Sabbath. Maybe instead of sleeping at night, you are up late scrolling through the Internet or working, but the Bible says God *"grants sleep to those he loves"* (Psalm 127:2). Maybe you've incorporated things into your routine that don't need to be there. Maybe God is calling you to release some commitments. Are there any activities or things that you are involved in that you know God didn't call you to do? If there is, daughter, I encourage you to go to your heavenly Father and surrender all those areas of your life to Him today. Release your own idea of what you think a successful life should look like and allow Him to show you what it truly feels like. Embrace the beauty of simply being His. Choose God's presence over performance and rest in the rhythms of His peace.

5

BEFORE YOU WERE

Who were you before you were born? That is who you truly are. Who are you beyond the titles? Who are you beyond the acclaim? Do you *really* know who you are? Before you were born into this world, you were somebody. So why would you go to this world to discover who you are? The only one who can show you who you truly are is your Creator, God Himself. He is the author of your life and your purpose. He is the one who gives us meaning and ascribes to us our authentic identity. Before you had any titles, before you even received your first name, you were already known in heaven.

Before I became a mother, before I became a wife, before I became an author, I was already God's daughter. This chapter will focus on identity, calling, and purpose while addressing some of the confusion surrounding these terms today.

First, your purpose is not what you do or how you do it. Your purpose is the reason why you were created. A lot of times, we make the mistake of thinking that our purpose has to be our occupation or our title. But the only way that you can know your purpose is to go to the Creator of that purpose.

GOD KNOWS WHY HE CREATED YOU

The person who created you is God Himself and only He knows the reason why He created you. To think about this by way of example, a seat belt has many characteristics and does several different things. A seat belt can stretch and it's very flexible, but was the seat belt created to stretch? No. Even though the seat belt does stretch, even though it can be called flexible, the seat belt wasn't created with the purpose of stretching. Instead, it was created to protect someone's life. That is its purpose, the reason why it was created.

So you may have different gifts. You may have different characteristics. You may have different talents. But those things are not your purpose. They may be unique qualities about you and aspects of your personality. They may be gifts that God has placed inside of you, but that doesn't always mean that is your specific purpose.

Let me give you another example. I am a writer. God has given me the gift of writing and the gift of communication. Writing is my passion. It is something that I wake up in the middle of the night desiring to do. I also stay up late at night just to write. So writing is something that I'm very passionate about ... but writing is not my purpose. My purpose is to share the gospel of Jesus Christ, to teach His Word. So even though I am a writer, even though people can describe me as a writer, or they ascribe that title to me, my true purpose is to share the gospel. Being a writer is not my purpose. I know that if I write a book that has nothing to do with sharing the gospel or leading people back to Christ, I may be operating in my gifting, but I'm not operating in my purpose.

God uses writing as an outlet for me to share the gospel and bring Him glory the same way that He uses many other gifts and things that I do. I don't just share the gospel through writing. I also share the gospel through my relationships, through speaking, and through creating.

So you have to know why God created you. What is the reason? Basically the question of purpose is, "Why am I here?"

Everything goes back to your purpose. You may have different gifts and talents. You may have different jobs. You may find yourself in different seasons or in different places in life, but your purpose is foundational. You'll see that when you're operating and flowing in your natural abilities, natural gifts, and talents.

If you keep going back to the core of it, ask yourself the question, "Why am I doing this?" When you are doing something that you're good at, it'll probably help you to pinpoint your purpose.

Ask yourself, "Why am I motivated to do this? What is my motivation? What inside of me makes me want to do it? What is my *why*? What is the reason?"

OUR SHARED PURPOSE

Everyone has a shared purpose to glorify God. Whatever we do, we should be glorifying God. As Christians, all of us also have a duty to share the gospel with people we know or encounter. But not everyone's purpose is to be a preacher, pastor, or Bible teacher. So ask yourself, "What is the specific thing that drives me?" Everyone's *why* is different, but I know my *why* is that I don't want people to go to hell. I want people to know the truth and to be saved. That drives everything that I do. So you have to find your why and that is the core of your purpose. No matter what you're doing, it's going to draw you back to, "Why am I doing this?" That is how I discovered my call as an evangelist.

It's important to realize that your purpose is not your calling. Purpose and calling are two different things. Your purpose is foundational. God created you with a purpose from the beginning of the earth. It is the foundation upon which He made you. Your purpose is set before you even start living your life, before you were even born.

Your calling, on the other hand, is usually something that happens during your life, even though God knows what He's going to call you to do in advance. It's literally God calling you. He's reaching out to you, telling you to do something specific. In fact, your calling can change in different seasons. Your purpose is innate, but your calling is something you must accept and answer if you wish to please God.

Your calling is a way to carry out your purpose. In this life, God has called me to be a mother. He's called me to be a wife. My family is my first ministry, and I'm able to minister to my family through my calling. It's something that God has called me to do and I had to accept this call and position in my life. My family is not my purpose. I'm not here because of my family, but this is a calling that I have while I am on earth, while also fulfilling the purpose that God has for me. I talked about how writing was one of my gifts. Being an author is also one of my callings. I know it's a calling because God literally told me, "I want you to write a book."

HEARING FROM THE HOLY SPIRIT

How do you recognize your calling? It is as if He is calling you on the phone but you feel it in your spirit. You feel the tug of the Holy Spirit giving you the grace to take on a specific role or action to complete an assignment. If you feel a nudge from the Holy Spirit, know that God is leading you and will give you confirmation if He has spoken a specific assignment on your life.

God will speak to you to have you do a specific thing or take on a new role. It is very specific and through that calling, you will further be able carry out your foundational purpose. For example, God has also called me to the platform of YouTube. I felt a strong urge to make YouTube videos. Carrying out the calling to start a YouTube channel helped me to carry out my purpose by reaching the nations with the gospel of Jesus Christ.

God has called me to the platform of YouTube but it is not my purpose. And there might be a season where I don't do YouTube videos. That just means it's a different season and maybe it's not my calling in that next season. But for this season, I am called to do YouTube videos and while I am doing that, I am fulfilling my purpose of sharing the gospel.

So when you think of calling, literally try to imagine what is that thing that God is trying to call you to if He could call you on the phone and tell you what to do. Or what is that thing that the Holy Spirit is nudging you to do on the inside? You are not called to do your purpose because your purpose is already inside of you. You just simply need to carry it out, from the inside.

The reason why you're here is already inside of you. You have to know your purpose and do what you are called to do. Your purpose is not something that you do. Your purpose is something that you know. It is your motivation. It is the reason why you were created. Your calling is something that you do because God has called you to do it.

Maybe your purpose is to get people to eat healthier and treat their bodies like a temple of God. So maybe God put you on this earth so that you can be an agent of change in the health industry. God can use different callings in your life at different seasons so that you can carry out your purpose through different stages and different ways. For instance, you may be called to write a book or a blog about health.

You may be called to go to medical school to become a doctor, but being a doctor may not necessarily be your purpose. You can discover your purpose by asking, "Why did God create me to be a doctor? Why am I a doctor? What am I supposed to do as a doctor? How am I called to bring glory to God as a doctor?" It may be something as simple as coming up with a new way to speak to patients and give people hope when they are hospitalized, or something as complex as finding a new breakthrough for a disease.

Everyone has a different purpose and specific reason for why they're here, but we can all share callings. Many people can be called to the medical field, but all those people can serve a different purpose.

We're all here for a unique reason. No one can do what you specifically were designed to do. That's why God made us all unique. That's why He made us different. We all have different fingerprints. We're all here with a specific and unique purpose.

Just because I'm called to be an author and you're called to be an author does not mean that we share the same purpose. Just because two people are called to be doctors does not mean that they share the same purpose. God could be calling them for different reasons. We all have a role to play. You can't compare your purpose to someone else's because although we may share the same callings, we may have a different purpose.

OUR SHARED CALLING IN CHRIST

We are the body of Christ, as the apostle Paul explains in his first letter to the Corinthians.

> *Just as a body, though one, has many parts, but all its many parts form one body, so it is with Christ. For we were all baptized by one Spirit so as to form one body—whether Jews or Gentiles, slave or free—and we were all given the one Spirit to drink. Even so the body is not made up of one part but of many. Now if the foot should say, "Because I am not a hand, I do not belong to the body," it would not for that reason stop*

being part of the body. And if the ear should say, "Because I am not an eye, I do not belong to the body," it would not for that reason stop being part of the body. If the whole body were an eye, where would the sense of hearing be? If the whole body were an ear, where would the sense of smell be? But in fact God has placed the parts in the body, every one of them, just as he wanted them to be. If they were all one part, where would the body be? As it is, there are many parts, but one body. The eye cannot say to the hand, "I don't need you!" And the head cannot say to the feet, "I don't need you!" On the contrary, those parts of the body that seem to be weaker are indispensable, and the parts that we think are less honorable we treat with special honor. And the parts that are unpresentable are treated with special modesty, while our presentable parts need no special treatment. But God has put the body together, giving greater honor to the parts that lacked it, so that there should be no division in the body, but that its parts should have equal concern for each other. If one part suffers, every part suffers with it; if one part is honored, every part rejoices with it.   (1 Corinthians 12:12–26)

Even the fingers on our hands share the same calling but each serves a different purpose. For example, the ring finger contributes to grip strength, the index finger is vital for pointing and precision tasks, the thumb is needed for precision and power grips, and so on. So just because they share the same calling doesn't mean that their purpose is the same. And we are like fingers on the hands of Jesus.

Sometimes you may see someone who shares your specific calling, and you may ask, "Am I unique? Do I have a purpose? Am I here for a reason?" And the answer is *yes*, God has put you here for a specific reason. We should all be confident in knowing that God has a specific plan and a purpose for our lives. There is a reason why you were created and part of the body of Christ. You may be a hand or a foot or an eye, but you should never compare yourself to another person.

The problem with the doctrine of doing that we discussed in chapter 3 is that living it out means we are doing things from a place of fear rather than a place of listening to God. We are doing things to perform for people rather than pleasing God. We should only be doing what God has called us to do. We shouldn't feel like we are doing things from a place of pressure and performance; what we are called to do for God should really come from a place of pleasure and praise. I take pleasure in obeying God, and whatever I do, I do it for the Lord, not for people. Colossians 3:23 says, "*Whatever you do, work at it with all your heart, as working for the Lord, not for human masters.*"

God wants us to be passionate and take pleasure in our calling. He wants us to have great energy and fervor when we are working unto Him. This leads me to my next point, the idea of following your passions.

FOLLOWING YOUR PASSIONS

Let's recap and break this down:

- Purpose: The reason why you're here
- Calling: What God desires you to do
- Passion: Your energy and effort
- Identity: Who you are

Your purpose is not always your passion. I want to address this because I mentioned that my passion is writing, but I also mentioned that writing is not my purpose. Some people say you can discover your purpose finding what you're passionate about, but that's not always true. I've heard so many stories of people who were passionate about something but God called them out of that and said, "This is not why you're here."

We are called to crucify *"the flesh with its passions and desires"* (Galatians 5:24), so passion does not always equate to calling. You can be placing energy and effort into something that God is not even calling you to do. God may very well call out your passion and let you know, "This is not what I've called you to do. This is not the purpose for which I've created you. Even though you're passionate about it, even though you want to do it, this is not what I want you to do."

I have a personal friend who is passionate about television broadcasting and wanted to be an actress. God said, "This is not your purpose. This is not why you're here and this will not bring Me glory. I know that you're passionate about it, but I've called you to start a health and wellness company. I've called you to help people honor Me with their bodies as temples of the Holy Spirit. I've called you to help fight sickness and disease and teach people how to live a healthier lifestyle."

We think we know what our purpose is. We think we want to do what we're passionate about. But after my friend crucified her acting passion and became obedient to God, she went forth, started her company, and became passionate about it. Sometimes you may not feel like doing what God has called you to do in the beginning, but the passion will come later because He knows the plan He has for you—and what's before you—better than you do. You can trust Him.

> *"For I know the plans I have for you,"* declares the LORD, *"plans to prosper you and not to harm you, plans to give you hope and a future."*   (Jeremiah 29:11)

When you step out and you're obedient to do what God has called you to do, the passion comes because it's already inside of you. You may not know it yet, but God already placed it there and built you for this. God created you for that specific thing.

I had an inclination of my purpose at a very young age. I knew that God had wanted me to speak and share the gospel when I was in middle school, but I ran away from this for a long time because I felt the heaviness and the weight of my purpose and what God was calling me to do. Now that I've walked into full-time ministry, I fully embrace my calling and my purpose and why I'm here on this earth. I absolutely love it and I can't see myself doing anything else. I want to see people healed. I want to see lives saved. I want to see people changed, delivered, and set free. But my form of ministry is not a typical one that others may expect. That is where identity comes in because we all have a unique and personal calling.

You don't discover your identity by "looking inside yourself," as some people may say. You discover your identity by looking to God and having a relationship with Him. I've heard teachings about doing some self-introspection, going on a vacation, or just "looking into yourself" to discover who you are. But sometimes our self is filled with a lot of junk. Sometimes we are filled with a lot of discontentment and comparison.

Our self is full of the flesh and when you're on a search for your identity, sometimes it's not enough to look into yourself. That may even be the last place that you should look. If we're not in the right place, if we're not in God, looking into ourselves may not show who we really are. But the Word of God serves as a mirror, reflecting who God created us to be.

Scripture says in James 1:23–24, "*Anyone who listens to the word but does not do what it says is like someone who looks at his face in a mirror and, after looking at himself, goes away and immediately forgets what he looks like.*"

WHAT GOD'S WORD SAYS YOU ARE

God has shown you what you look like; He has shown you who you are in His Word. If you are struggling with identity or if you have forgotten who you are, let me remind you:

- You are accepted. (Romans 15:7)
- You are chosen. (John 15:16)
- You are free. (Galatians 4:7)
- You are forgiven. (1 John 1:9)
- You are a child of God. (John 1:12)
- You are made in God's image. (Genesis 1:27)
- You are precious to God. (Isaiah 43:4)
- You are an heir of God. (Romans 8:17)

The list can go on and on.

The truth's at the core of your identity in Christ. When you cling to it, God will begin to reveal to you more intimate and unique details about who you are, such as your personality, quirks, and gifts. Your life experiences and circumstances may change, but the core of who you are will always remain because it is hidden in God, the one who is *the Alpha and the Omega* (Revelation 1:8), *the same yesterday and today and forever* (Hebrews 13:8).

God knows why He created you. Ask everyone on this earth who has created something—every artist, every author, every builder, every inventor—"Why did you create this?" and they will always have an answer for you. They all created it with a purpose in mind. God is the only One you can go to to know your purpose. This involves having a relationship with Him.

If you currently don't know your purpose or your calling, that does not mean that you don't have them, nor does it mean that you are outside of God's will. Don't let the enemy lie to you and cause you to feel inadequate.

I was walking in my purpose before I knew what my purpose was. Right now, you are operating in your purpose because God is the one working in you to carry it out. Scripture says, *"And I am certain that God, who began the good work within you, will continue his work until it is finally finished on the day when Christ Jesus returns"* (Philippians 1:6 NLT).

If you have a relationship with God and you continue to abide in Him and remain in Him, you are operating on purpose. Just simply *be*! Isn't it a breath of fresh air to know that from simply being and remaining in the Lord, God is working in and through you? Honey, you are living out your purpose. You are living out your life. You may not know it but you're living out your purpose at that job you're at right now.

You may not know why you're at that job, but if God blessed you with that job, there is a purpose for you being there. God is preparing you. He's teaching you fruits of the Spirit for the next season that He's calling you to. He's teaching you patience, kindness, love, and self-control.

I went through many seasons in life where I just did not get it. I thought, "Why am I here right now? God, what are You doing? Why are we doing this? I just want to know my purpose and I want to live it out and I want to walk in my purpose." As long as you're walking with God and abiding by His Word and truth, that is walking in your purpose. All the pieces of the puzzle are going to come together and it's going to make sense in due season.

Now that I know my purpose, I can look back and I can say:

+ Oh, that's what You were doing in that season.
+ Oh, that's what I was learning at that place.
+ Oh, that's why I had to go through that.
+ Oh, that's why I had to heal through that.

I see how God was putting it all together. I see how He was working things out for my good. The Bible says, *"All things work together for good to those who love God, to those who are the called according to His purpose"* (Romans 8:28 NKJV).

You need to be content in the season that you're in and know that it's going to work out for your good. You are in purpose. You no longer have to compare your journey to someone else who looks like they're walking out their purpose. More than focusing on doing what God has called you to do, always remember to simply *be* who He's already purposed you to be.

GIVE GOD YOUR "YES"

Just wake up every morning and give God your yes. It's not about performing; it's about aligning with His perfect will. That yes can mean being faithful to your role as a stay-at-home mom. God may be saying, "I want you to just focus on raising your kids in this season." That's your yes. You are walking in your purpose.

You don't need to start a business. You don't need to go out and start a ministry. You don't have to do something big for the world to see in order to feel validated or like you're walking out your purpose. You don't need the acclaim of man. You don't need an award. You don't need a title for you to feel like you're walking in your purpose. If you have a relationship with the Creator and if you're doing what He tells you to do, you are walking in your purpose. It's just a matter of time until your purpose is revealed to you. God will reveal it in the right season. Sometimes He doesn't reveal it to you too early because you would run away from it.

If God had told me my purpose in middle school or high school, I don't know where I would be today because I was already running away. I wasn't sure what my purpose was; I was just running away from what He called me to do to begin with. I didn't even follow the basic instructions first, let alone realize what my purpose was. So I wasn't ready to hear it. I couldn't even handle the simple instructions. What God wanted me to do in that season was simply abide in Him, grow, build a strong foundation of faith, and simply *be*.

6

PEOPLE-PLEASING

This chapter takes a deeper look into the snare of people-pleasing. I refer to it as a snare because it creeps up on you subtly. It is camouflaged as a good thing, especially since much of our Christian theology tells us to be kind and loving toward people. Yet as always, the enemy can find a way to twist the truth, so we wind up operating under the false pretense that we are helping someone else when it's really just hurting us and others in the long run.

The Bible says, *"Fear of man will prove to be a snare, but whoever trusts in the LORD is kept safe"* (Proverbs 29:25).

So who do you fear, God or people? Whatever you fear is what controls you. You can tell what people are controlled by based on the decisions they make when it comes to others. For example, I've seen people enable someone's destructive, addictive, and unhealthy habits, thinking that they are helping that person. They buy into the promises that the person gives them, such as, "This is the last time," or "I just need your help." They will bail the person out or enable that person to fall right back into their trap of weakness and addiction. While this person is controlled by their addiction and their unhealthy habits, the enabler opens the door to be controlled by that same spirit. It is a spiritual principle that you reap what you sow. (See Galatians 6:7.)

If you are constantly sowing dysfunction or lending money to someone who is an addict, then you are inviting that same type of dysfunction into your life. If that person is controlled by the lust of the flesh, you are feeding into that same type of demonic control and form of bondage. Bondage is the reason why some people keep showing up time after time despite the damaging effects. They are people-pleasing; they don't know how to say *no* and they are being influenced by another spirit that is not the Spirit of God. That is a dangerous place to be, trapped in the fear of man and the perpetual toxic cycle of pleasing people.

Why should you fear man? Scripture says, *"Don't be afraid of those who want to kill your body; they cannot touch your soul. Fear only God, who can destroy both soul and body in hell"* (Matthew 10:28 NLT).

WHAT DOES GOD DESIRE FOR YOU?

I personally have witnessed how people-pleasing was a hindrance to my ministry and the flow of the Holy Spirit. Now, any decision that I make related to my ministry has to be because God has instructed me, not because people have pressured me. What may seem good to people may not be the will that God desires for you. I remember one time when God called me to host a conference. Back then, I would invite different speakers and people to participate based on who I believed the people wanted to hear or listen to. That was a dangerous mindset to have because it is the tendency of the flesh to please people when it comes to ministry.

A time is coming when people will no longer listen to sound and wholesome teaching. They will follow their own desires and will look for teachers who will tell them whatever their itching ears want to hear. (2 Timothy 4:3 NLT)

Though I did not invite anyone to speak at the conference who was teaching false doctrine, I was still operating from the root of caring what people think and trying to go with what would be popular or accepted at the time for that kind of event, which was a grave mistake. Now, if I ever invite a speaker to an event, I don't care about their popularity or status. I would rather invite someone unknown and unpopular who has a pure love for God than someone with a large following on social media yet operates in pride and does not bear the fruit of the Spirit.

I should have known that God didn't want me to invite any guest speakers to this particular conference at all. Actually, He wanted me to host the conference solo, but I was so caught up with how other people's conferences looked, I felt I needed to have a certain line-up and fancy ministry flyer. Well, the keynote speaker who I invited that year was not God's choice. I know that deep down inside, God had desired for me to step up to the plate and do what He has called me to do, despite what I thought people wanted and desired out of a Christian event and conference. That is why it is so dangerous to compare your path to others. Just because other people operate a certain way does not make it God's will for you. Though people were impacted positively through the event and God still showed up for the sake of the people, I know that it was not the result He would have desired. In that moment, God had called me to step up to my calling, but people-pleasing and fear of man had me running away from it like Jonah in the Bible.

JONAH LEARNED TO FEAR THE LORD

Jonah was someone who ran away from God; he was disobedient because he lacked the fear of the Lord. But after being swallowed up in the belly of a great fish, God gracefully instilled the fear of the Lord within him. It was then that Jonah repented, the fish spit him out onto dry land, and he went to preach to the city of Nineveh. (See Jonah 2–3.) The fear of the Lord is a gift that God sparked in Jonah's life by allowing him to be swallowed up by a great fish after a terrible storm.

Proverbs 14:27 says, *"The fear of the LORD is a fountain of life, turning a person from the snares of death."*

God knew that Jonah was trying to hide and run away from Him by going the wrong way. When Jonah's near-death experience made him fear the Lord, it put him back on track to fulfilling his purpose and answering the call on his life. Because he went to the city of Nineveh and preached against it, the people humbled themselves with a fast, and God relented by not destroying the city as He had originally intended.

I too have had some near-death experiences and instances when God instilled a healthy fear of the Lord within me. I remember one year when I went against the instruction of the Holy Spirit to travel and participate in some Halloween activities. I know that God instructed me not to go, but I wanted to do my own thing, and in that season in my life, I was backsliding and living my own life in college, doing what I wanted to do.

On the way back after the event, I got into a bad car accident that was a close call. If it wasn't for me screaming, "Jesus!" and Him performing a miracle to save me, I don't think I would be here today. God spared my life at that moment. It is after moments like these that I truly repent from my ways and turn back to God.

That instance was a wake-up call for me because I recognized the fragility of life and truly did not want to waste my life walking in disobedience. At the time, I was trying to fit in with my college friends and wanted to be a part of their worldly celebrations even though I knew this did not honor God.

Though I am not perfect, God always gets me back on track when I choose to stop giving into people-pleasing and peer pressure and instead allow my reverence for the Father to truly lead my life decisions and actions.

Since maturing in the Lord, I don't invite guest speakers to my events lightly; I always pray and ask the Holy Spirit for confirmation that it's okay. I have hosted several conferences and ministry events by myself without any crazy or fancy lineup, just me and the Holy Spirit. These events have been filled with God's power, presence, testimonies of deliverance, and freedom. Of course, God has given me covering and aligned me with a group of prayer warriors to pray and assist at my events, which is necessary. I have realized that what God has called me to do will not look like the traditional form of ministry that people are used to, and that's fine. We can accomplish more through obedience and the Spirit of God than we can accomplish by following a worldly template made by man. Your calling does not have to look like someone else's.

RULERS CAN BE PEOPLE PLEASERS TOO

Even kings are not immune to people-pleasing. God had instructed King Saul to destroy the city of Amalek and kill everything, including the animals, women, infants, and children. (See 1 Samuel 15:3.) Yet Saul disobeyed God and spared the Amalekites' king, Agag, along with their best sheep, cattle, and lambs. (See verse 9.) Then the Lord told the prophet Samuel that He regretted anointing Saul as king.

Samuel went to Saul and rebuked him saying, *"For rebellion is as the sin of witchcraft, and stubbornness is as iniquity and idolatry. Because you have rejected the word of the LORD, He also has rejected you from being king"* (1 Samuel 15:23 NKJV). Saul responded, *"I have sinned, for I have transgressed the commandment of the* LORD *and your words,* **because I feared the people and obeyed their voice**" (verse 24 NKJV).

Saul regretted giving in to his subjects' wishes but that didn't change anything. God still rejected him as king and soon afterward had Samuel anoint David as the new king.

This biblical example illustrates the fact that when you are disobedient to God due to people-pleasing and the fear of man, you can actually lose the position and anointing that God intended for you to have. If you are more concerned with how people see you rather than how God sees you, you are playing with fire. That is the thing with labels and position—all of that is temporary and can be taken away at any moment if God chooses to humble us. Saul was a king, having one of the most highly esteemed labels that a man can have on this earth. Still even then, we must remember, it is God who removes kings and set up kings.

We should never place too much confidence in a position or title, humbly knowing that at any moment, God can take it away. If you feel like you have an unhealthy tie to a certain title, place, or position in your life, I encourage you to surrender that on an altar of sacrifice to the Lord. It's important to make sure that these things don't get to our heads and become idols in our life, but we always keep God in his rightful place of Lord over our life. Circumstances change and people will change, but God is unchanging. What I've learned and seen is that people will love you and praise you in one season of life, but then they will hate you and try to cancel you in the next. That is why your hope and value should never be dependent on people, but on God alone.

Saul was actually not God's pick for a king to begin with. There is a lesson in how King Saul was appointed because He was the people's choice and not God's choice. They wanted a man to lead them rather than the Lord, and Saul was tall in stature and charismatic. "*The people begged for a king, and God gave them Saul son of Kish, a man of the tribe of Benjamin, who reigned for forty years"* (Acts 13:21 NLT).

The people begged for a king, and God gave them what they wanted to demonstrate that we often don't know what is best for our own good. When God says *no* to you, it's because He loves you and has the best plan for your life, His plan. God wants us to know and practice how to also say *no* to people, even when we are being pressured, coerced, tempted, or bribed. God gives us the power to resist temptation and make the right decision.

> *No temptation has overtaken you except what is common to mankind. And God is faithful; he will not let you be tempted beyond what you can bear. But when you are tempted, he will also provide a way out so that you can endure it.*
> (1 Corinthians 10:13)

God wants us to understand that anything outside of His plan for us will ultimately lead to destruction. I thank God that He doesn't give us our desires, but rather He renews our hearts to have His desires, and then He gives us the desires of our heart when we delight ourselves in Him. (See Psalm 37:4.)

THE ENEMY CAN KEEP YOU BUSY

The enemy's goal is to keep you busy, distracted, and saying *yes* to any and everything that can take your focus away from God. You may not have noticed it before, but busyness is actually a form of temptation. It could be tempting to please people because we want to feel accepted, liked, and loved. It could be tempting to take on more responsibilities when we think that it could help further our status and position. It could be tempting to start more projects, more businesses, do more ministry, and be more active without truly asking God if that's what He desires. Maybe you like the attention that you get when it seems like you're being productive, but is it really fruitful? Productivity does not equate to fruitfulness.

God really had to teach me to build some fortitude in this area and learn how to stand firm on my word and say *no* when my flesh really wanted to say *yes*. Then the Lord took me through a spiritual process that I call "resistance training" to really break free from people-pleasing.

If you are familiar with the world of health and wellness and you've ever been on a journey of physical fitness and transformation, you may be familiar with the term "resistance training," also known as strength training or weight training. This is a type of exercise that increases muscle strength, endurance, and size by making muscles contract against resistance. Resistance can come from your own body weight or equipment like free weights, weight machines, or resistance bands. In simple terms, resistance training features exercises designed to make you stronger.

Once I started rejecting the urge to people-please, I noticed that I came across a lot of resistance, though not literal. I realized that once I committed to the process of learning how to simply *be*, I began to receive some backlash from the communities that once embraced me. Where I was once celebrated, I felt like I was now just being tolerated. It seemed that when I was people-pleasing, I was promoted and accepted, but once I made the shift into simply being, I was misunderstood and rejected.

People didn't understand why I was doing things differently or not even doing some things at all. It seems that they didn't want the raw and authentic sides of me; they preferred the performance based and curated sides of me. I started to lose friends and followers when I stopped giving people what they expected of me. I was faced with the test of remaining authentic or falling back into my people-pleasing ways. I was coming up against resistance, but God showed me that this spiritual resistance training was only a test and exercise to make me stronger.

You can't serve God and be in bondage to what people think of you. You can't be afraid of people and their reactions; we must only fear God. It's normal to face resistance when you start swimming in the opposite direction of the natural current. The enemy will lie to you, mess with your mind, and make you think that something is wrong with you, but nothing is wrong. You are in a vulnerable space because you have stripped yourself of all the things you used to fall back on that once made you feel safe. The approval, applause, titles, status, busyness, and familiar places are all now gone. When you face pushback and resistance, will you run back to those old places and your old ways of doing things? Or are you willing to allow God to do the new thing in you? It is time to break free from the mold that comes with the fear of man by refusing to compromise your authenticity, purpose, and identity for the sake of worldly acceptance and conformity.

FOLLOWING GOD'S STANDARD

As daughters of God, we must realize that though we are in this world, we are not *of* the world. Rather than bending to the culture and worldly standards, we should allow for God's standard to be revealed in and through us, no longer allowing society to dictate our path and journey in life but allowing ourselves to break out of the box of man's expectations and fully surrender to God's perfect will for us.

That is why I want to talk a little bit more about what it truly means to be free. What does it look like to be free from people, free from expectations, free from legalism, *free to simply be*. Because the best place to be in life is free. You show up differently when God is the only One who owns you and that's how it should be.

I was never able to fully walk in what God had for me because for over the past ten years, I was always bound to something. That was the enemy's tactic to keep me stuck, going through the motions and reliving the same cycles, season after season, year after year. Even when it seemed that I would break free from one thing, I would be bound by another. It wasn't until God opened my eyes to reveal to me the tactic of the enemy to keep me distracted that I finally turned the page and broke away from the curse of bad habits and bad decisions.

I promised myself that this was the last time I was starting from square one again. I refused to be like the Israelites who God delivered from slavery in Egypt but became bound by something else when they got into the wilderness. They became bound by the open door of their idolatry. That is why we must always be alert. Even after we pass some tests and God sets us free in one area, that does not mean that we have arrived and that we won't get tested in another area. Scripture tells us:

> *Stay alert! Watch out for your great enemy, the devil. He prowls around like a roaring lion, looking for someone to devour.*   (1 Peter 5:8 NLT)

This is what happened to me. Like the Israelites who went around the same mountain for forty years, I spent ten years of my life bound because I wasn't alert and aware of the enemy's tactics to keep me bound time after time. I always wondered why my life was like a roller coaster, with high highs and low lows. I would pass tests and get a moment of relief and breakthrough, but then the enemy would find my blind spots and catch me from another angle or in another area that I wasn't aware of. Then before I knew it, I would be right back in the ditch I thought that God had rescued me from. It never made sense to me and it was hard to understand while I was in it. Now when I look back at those times, I understand.

FROM ONE BONDAGE TO ANOTHER

First, I was bound to people for years. I was worried about what they thought of me; I struggled with rejection and wanted to be liked and accepted. Then I met a mentor who pointed out this weakness in me and helped me to overcome it. I became free from caring what people think … but then fell into the next trap. I went from people-pleasing to idolizing one person, the same person who helped me to get over people-pleasing. Now I was idolizing her and most of my life actions at the time were in bondage to her approval of me. Then when God led me to break off that relationship, I was free.

For a moment, I was relieved, but then I turned to self. For so long, I had been in bondage to people externally. I felt like I missed out on pleasing myself internally. So I became more interested in pursuing *my own* dreams and desires, thinking that was the solution that I needed. I wanted to be promoted and become the "best version of myself," so I turned to this world's system, looking for acceptance and trying to play by their rules regarding how I should look, walk, speak, and present myself. In trying to promote myself, I lost myself to the point of not even being able to recognize who I was anymore. When I didn't get the result of self-promotion that I desired, I returned to square one, back where I started even years before the people-pleasing, the first thing God ever delivered me from: food addiction and gluttony. I started overeating, eating out of emotion because I felt a loss of control. I felt like I was slipping away, so I started eating away.

This point was the pinnacle of my journey, my defining moment. Would I go back to the place of enslavement that God delivered me from? Would I return to my form of Egypt? Or would I finally surrender, as a servant of God, bound only to Christ, dying to self, so I could truly finally be free and live the life God always intended me to live?

To be true followers of Christ, the Bible says we must deny ourselves.

Then Jesus said to His disciples, "If anyone desires to come after Me, let him deny himself, and take up his cross, and follow Me."   (Matthew 16:24 NKJV)

This is the beauty of *being* more like Christ and less like you. This is where I am today while writing this book. I have decided to follow Jesus *fully* and I will not go back to the bondage God brought me through. I will not look for another idol to put in His place. I will not be ensnared by the fear of man. No, I am choosing to move forward in pleasing my God, the One who has always been faithful, the One who has never changed on me. He is the same yesterday, today, and tomorrow, and He is worth my entire life. I have made the decision to deny myself, carry my cross, and live for the One who gave His life for me. Jesus is more than life to me. Ten years in the wilderness is more than enough. I am laying it all down to experience the beauty of *being* in the promised land God has set before me.

For to me, to live is Christ and to die is gain.
                              (Philippians 1:21)

7

MORE THAN ENOUGH

In this chapter, I want us to abandon the benchmarks that we set or accept for ourselves and instead consider the standard set by God's Word. It actually may surprise you to find out that some of the things we think God wants from us are things He doesn't care about, and the things that He actually cares about are the areas we should truly be focused on.

> "For my thoughts are not your thoughts, neither are your ways my ways," declares the LORD. "As the heavens are higher than the earth, so are my ways higher than your ways and my thoughts than your thoughts." (Isaiah 55:8–9)

We have our own ideas about what's important and what should be highly esteemed, but from this Scripture, we realize that what we think may actually not be in alignment with God. God's ways and thoughts are always higher than what we may have in mind ourselves. The thing is, God does not look at what people look at or consider the things that people consider. Recall that when the prophet Samuel was getting ready to anoint David as king, God told Samuel, "*The Lord does not look at the things people look at. People look at the outward appearance, but the Lord looks at the heart*" (1 Samuel 16:7).

As people, we often judge others based on their outward appearance and how things look on the outside—by the brand of clothing that someone wears, the type of car that they drive, how much money they earn, and so on. Unfortunately, we feed into these kinds of narratives when we buy into this performance-based behavior and show favoritism toward people who look like they are of a certain status or try to present ourselves in a certain way to control how people perceive us. The Bible speaks against such favoritism in the church.

> *My dear brothers and sisters, how can you claim to have faith in our glorious Lord Jesus Christ if you favor some people over others? For example, suppose someone comes into your meeting dressed in fancy clothes and expensive jewelry, and another comes in who is poor and dressed in dirty clothes. If you give special attention and a good seat to the rich person, but you say to the poor one, "You can stand over there, or else sit on the floor"—well, doesn't this discrimination show that your judgments are guided by evil motives?*
>
> (James 2:1–4 NLT)

Many of us are guilty of the sin of showing favoritism or pre-judging someone out of the wrong motives. It could be as simple as judging someone based on the amount of likes and followers they have on social media rather than considering their spiritual fruit, which is the rightful standard for judging given to us by the Word of God. (See Matthew 7:16–20.) We have churches with VIP sections and a strong celebrity culture in the church because we have allowed the world's culture to influence church culture. Yet the Bible tells us:

Live in harmony with one another. Do not be proud, but be willing to associate with people of low position. Do not be conceited. (Romans 12:16)

SEEKING A KINGDOM CULTURE

God is calling us to turn from the practices of the world and even go beyond the practices of the church, so that we might be renewed in our minds and operate out of kingdom culture. Church culture is just as bad worldly culture when it is tainted with religiosity and hypocrisy. God desires us to carry out His kingdom culture and purpose on this earth. That is why the Word of God says, *"Your kingdom come, your will be done, on earth as it is in heaven"* (Matthew 6:10). God's kingdom come is His desire and will to accomplish while we are on this earth.

The kingdom of God is the manifestation of the kingdom of heaven. If you think of what heaven will be like, it is God's will and desire to also bring that forth in the earth realm. In heaven, it is all about unity. Every tribe, nation, and tongue will be joined together as one. Your skin tone, your race, background, status, labels, titles, or any of that will not matter. We will all just be humbled and thankful to be in God's presence, worshipping and praising Him together. None of us will be able to boast or have pride in the Lord's presence. Do you remember what happened to Satan when he had pride? He fell from heaven.

Unity is one of the key components to fulfilling God's ultimate will and plan. We must learn how to live in unity now while on earth because that is how we will be living with each other for all eternity. It is not God's will for us to constantly live in a place of comparison, looking down on each other or being concerned with things such as status and position. The Bible makes it clear that we are to be unified as one body.

> *As a prisoner for the Lord, then, I urge you to live a life worthy of the calling you have received. Be completely humble and gentle; be patient, bearing with one another in love. Make every effort to keep the unity of the Spirit through the bond of peace. There is one body and one Spirit, just as you were called to one hope when you were called; one Lord, one faith, one baptism; one God and Father of all, who is over all and through all and in all.* (Ephesians 4:1–6)

We live in a society that has so much competition, that says there can only be one winner. Unfortunately, this gives us an unhealthy perspective as we navigate through life. We see life as either you win or you lose. We struggle with things like jealousy and discontentment because we feel like if someone else is winning, it must mean *we* are losing. We feel if someone else is successful, that must mean something is wrong with us or we are not doing enough. We've become such a self-centered and individualistic society, everything has become about me, me, me—iPhone, iPad, my truth, my this, my that. Yet truthfully speaking, this is antichrist in nature and goes against the kingdom.

The kingdom of God is oneness, unity, and family. From the beginning of time, God created the family, and people lived in the context of tribes, clans, and kin. Due to the onset of technology and the widespread nature of sin on the earth, people have given into divisions and dissensions, causing them to fend for themselves rather than fending and fighting for their families, relationships, and keeping the peace. We are so quick to drop people when we feel like they "no longer serve us," although we are the ones called to serve others. We are so quick to quit a relationship because we do not want to communicate, develop patience, and bear with one another in love. We rush to divorce, ghost someone, and move on to the next person.

DESIGNED FOR LIFE IN A FAMILY

These individualistic and narcissistic tendencies are causing more people going through life feeling alone, depressed, and anxious. We were never designed to live life alone. God wants us to live in a family. Marriage is an institution of God, and that is why the enemy is so strategic in attacking marriage and family. Satan knows that these institutions are not only the backbone of a healthy society on this earth but are also a reflection of true kingdom culture and God's ultimate will for humanity that will be fully revealed when Christ returns for His bride, the church, without spot or blemish, and we live together in unity for the rest of eternity.

If the enemy can get you to focus solely on self and feed you the lie that the success of people around you means that God has forgotten about you, or you're not doing enough, he can trick you into thinking that you'll never be enough. You will have this insatiable desire to achieve, set goals, and garner more experiences for yourself, but it will *never* be enough.

I am here to tell you right now that you don't need any of that stuff. *In Christ, you are more than enough.* You have more and you *are* more through Christ. And I am not just saying this because it's a catchy saying because you've probably heard it said before. But I am saying this because it is the truth. Someone else's win does not equate to your loss. When we adopt the mind of Christ and realize that we are one and we are all in this together, a win for anyone in the body is a win for all of the body. We need one another.

> *In all these things we are more than conquerors through him who loved us.*   (Romans 8:37)

Unfortunately, many women feel like once they reach a certain stage or position in life, they will finally be worthy, they will finally be enough. Once they get married ... once they have children ... once they get a job promotion ... once their business takes off... We often work toward achieving a specific benchmark to finally feel validated.

IF YOU'VE HAD ENOUGH TRYING TO *BE* ENOUGH

Enough of that! Enough striving for acceptance or validation. Enough placing your worth in titles or circumstances. Enough of striving to be enough when all God requires of you is to simply *be*! More importantly, God is enough, and the sacrifice Jesus made on the cross for you is more than enough. You don't have to add anything to it, and you can't take anything away from it.

Rather than operating under pressure, fear, and a scarcity mindset, we must bear the fruit of the Spirit as beloved daughters of God. We can live from a place of peace, faith, and abundance through Christ.

Many people struggle with the fear of failure, and it's something I'm familiar with too. One of the things I realized about myself is that I would take failure and rejection really hard. When I failed at something, it literally did something to my psyche and shattered my confidence. I could be on cloud nine, but let me experience major disappointment, and it would take the wind from beneath my sails. I don't know why, but failure seemed to be a thief in my life. Not just a thief of joy, but a bandit to my identity. When I accept failure as an option, it robs me of my true identity and I cease from living and operating as a victor through Christ.

I begin to self-sabotage and I wonder, "How do I stop this roller coaster of emotions eating away at my peace of mind? How do I live with the constant bad reports, negative results, losses, and offenses? Why can't I just seem to catch a break?"

PUT ON THE FULL ARMOR OF GOD

When the harsh realities are constantly chipping away at your faith, how can you fight back and keep your place? How can you stand your ground when you feel beat to the ground? Here is what the Holy Spirit says through the apostle Paul:

> *Finally, be strong in the Lord and in his mighty power. Put on the full armor of God, so that you can take your stand against the devil's schemes. For our struggle is not against flesh and blood, but against the rulers, against the authorities, against the powers of this dark world and against the spiritual forces of evil in the heavenly realms. Therefore put on the full armor of God, so that when the day of evil comes, you may be able to **stand your ground**, and after you have done everything, to stand. Stand firm then, with the belt of truth buckled around your waist, with the breastplate of righteousness in place, and with your feet fitted with the readiness that comes from the gospel of peace. In addition to all this, take up the shield of faith, with which you can extinguish all the flaming arrows of the evil one. Take the helmet of salvation and the sword of the Spirit, which is the word of God. And pray in the Spirit on all occasions with all kinds of prayers and requests. With this in mind, be alert and always keep on praying for all the Lord's people.* (Ephesians 6:10–18)

You only fail if you give in. Don't ever back down from a fight, but make sure you are fully equipped and prepared for this fight of life. In World Wrestling Entertainment (WWE), the fight isn't over until one fighter has tapped out (given up) or their opponent has them held down for a certain amount of time, so that the referee blows the whistle and calls the winner. In spiritual warfare, you have an unfair advantage because the great Referee is on your side and He controls the time. Your fight of life is not over until

God says it's over. We don't wrestle against flesh and blood like they do at the WWE conventions, but we are in a spiritual fight and battle for our souls. As long as you refuse to tap out, as long as you never give up and never give in, you will overcome by God's mighty power.

Many WWE wrestlers win a belt after their fights, but God has already given you a belt, *"the belt of truth"* (Ephesians 6:14). Before you even entered the wrestling ring of life, you already won! You already have the victory belt around your waist. The truth of God's Word says that Jesus already won the victory over death, hell, and the grave when He died on calvary and rose again for you and me.

> *But thanks be to God! He gives us the victory through our Lord Jesus Christ.* (1 Corinthians 15:57)

> *For whatever is born of God overcomes the world. And this is the victory that has overcome the world—our faith.* (1 John 5:4 NKJV)

BE CONTENT TO BE YOURSELF

Apart from the fear of failure, another thing I struggled with on my journey of being while becoming was finding contentment. I struggled with being completely honest and content with where I am and who I am today, right now, in this moment.

It's easy to *be yourself* when you love yourself. But what happens when you love the future ideal of yourself more than the current version of yourself? Or what happens if you love the past version of yourself better than the current version? What happens when you don't quite show up in real life in the same way that you envision yourself showing up in your dreams? Can you still look in the mirror and be happy with what you see, while honestly admitting,

"God is still working on me"? What happens when your potential is still being processed?

If I can be honest, that is where I found myself. Even as I write this book, I wonder why I don't always look like the version of me that God talks about in the Bible. Why don't I always look like the version of me that's *"the head and not the tail,"* above only, not beneath (Deuteronomy 28:13 NKJV)? Why don't I always feel like the righteous version of me who is *"as bold as a lion"* (Proverbs 28:1)? Or the version of me who is a victor, not a victim? If I'm being honest, sometimes I do feel like the victim. Sometimes I fail and feel weak, frail, and tossed around by life.

You may be wondering, "How dare she say these things in a Christian book?" Because I have taught people that words are powerful, and you will reap what you speak. Similar to messages that some have heard from some Christian movements, we have been conditioned to speak what we'd like to believe rather than the reality we perceive. Many of us have been taught the fearmongering doctrine surrounding the use of words, emphasizing the *power* of word curses rather than the redemptive power of God.

GOD'S POWER IS MORE THAN ENOUGH

I want to remind you that God's power is more than enough, even in the moments when reality is too pervasive to ignore. Even in the moments when our faith is being tested, there is still One greater than the test. Being honest about the condition of your mind, body, soul, and spirit does not mean you are accepting defeat. But it means you can invite God into your areas of weakness, learn from your mistakes, and grow.

For instance, individuals going through rehabilitation who may be suffering from a substance abuse problem are taken through a twelve-step program for healing and recovery. The first step is to *admit* that you are powerless over your addiction and need help. Though the twelve-step program is a secular curriculum used in many rehab facilities in the world, I've found that much of the process is biblically sound. Admission or confession is always a great way to initiate a process of healing and true growth and transformation. It takes a level of honesty to admit that there is a problem.

James 5:16 (NLT) says, "*Confess your sins to each other and pray for each other so that you may be healed. The earnest prayer of a righteous person has great power and produces wonderful results.*"

In this era of New Age doctrine and manifestation teachings, some think that results come from the confession or repetition of certain words or phrases. According to the Scripture above, confession with the intent to produce certain results is not a biblically sound practice because the humble posture of prayer is missing from the equation. It says that the *prayer* of a righteous person has power and produces results. It does not say that the constant *confession* of the righteous person does this.

Confession should be used to initiate us into earnest prayer and submission to the Lord. It should not be used as a form of control over our own lives, but rather as an open door of surrender to God. When we use confession as a way to manifest or control our own lives, we are in direct rebellion to the will of the Father who Himself desires to be Lord over our lives. The Bible says, "*Rebellion is as sinful as witchcraft*" (1 Samuel 15:23 NLT). People may not realize it, but dabbling in manifestation and New Age affirmation practices, when not biblically rooted, can open the door to the spirit of witchcraft in their life.

More powerful than mere confession, when we confess our sin to another, it positions us to pray in agreement with someone else versus praying by ourselves. To confess to someone else takes honesty, vulnerability, and humility.

It takes you acknowledging and admitting your area of weakness. You have to put all pride aside and remove any facade of perfection that many of us like to hide behind. That is how this type of prayer is powerful, effective, and able to produce wonderful results. Not only are you humbling yourself and giving God more room to move, but you are standing in unity and agreement on His Word, which is a spiritual guarantee to usher in His presence. Jesus says, *"For where two or three gather in my name, there am I with them"* (Matthew 18:20).

When we are constantly forward-thinking and in a mindset of *becoming* what's next or becoming "a better version of myself," as some might say, it's almost as if we are failing to acknowledge and accept the reality of where we are today. Sometimes the honesty of it all is the hardest part, but we need the raw truth if we truly want to live fully and authentically.

BE YOUR AUTHENTIC SELF!

People don't come to Christ through who you want to become or who you pretend to be. People come to Christ through who you authentically are in Him daily. They come to Christ through watching your everyday life and hearing your testimony of what God brought you through to bring you to where you are today. Sometimes we forget about that. We forget that we are currently living the dream of our past selves. You are not the same person today that you were yesterday. You are living some answered prayers. You are a testament to God's goodness, favor, and grace. That fact that you are even still here today, alive and breathing, is a miracle in itself.

Have you taken the time to settle in that? Have you paused and looked around to see where God has brought you compared to where you were? Do you need to be reminded of the times when God saved you, protected you, and pulled you out of a pit? That is the beautiful person God wants you to be, who He has made you to be right now. That is the version of you the world is looking at and the version of you that the world can relate to. They want to know that you've been through something. They want to see how you still love God and choose to serve Him even as you are currently navigating life.

The most real person I know is Jesus. He came into this world as a baby in a manger. The first version of Him that we met was the most humble, lowly, and helpless one. He could have come as His most glorified version, seated at the right hand of the Father in Heaven, but no, He chose to stoop down to our level and come as a mortal man. He did this to save us. He did this to relate to us and let us know that we are not alone. Everything we walked through, He walked through as well.

> For we do not have a High Priest who cannot sympathize with our weaknesses, but was in all points tempted as we are, yet without sin.   (Hebrews 4:15 NKJV)

Jesus can sympathize with any hardship or temptation you've experienced in life. He understands. Not only is He real and relatable, but He is also very honest. On the night He was betrayed, Jesus went to the garden of Gethsemane to pray. He did not go alone; He brought His disciples with Him to stand in agreement, demonstrating to us the importance of unity in prayer. Jesus was at a weak moment in His life. Yes, I just said that, and you know what, He started His night of prayer by being completely honest about it as well. Even Jesus was able to make some honest admissions.

He told His disciples, *"My soul is overwhelmed with sorrow to the point of death"* (Matthew 26:38). He did not say, "I am blessed and highly favored!" in an attempt to manifest a different emotion or outcome in His situation. Unfortunately, that is what a lot of modern-day Christians would do in response to a situation like this, "name it and claim it" as they say. But Jesus felt the weight and reality of the situation, was honest about it, and proceeded to pray. Then He went on to confess to the Lord, *"O My Father, if it is possible, let this cup pass from Me; nevertheless, not as I will, but as You will"* (Matthew 26:39 NKJV). There was a moment in time when Jesus Himself questioned God's plan. He wondered, "Is there any other possible way we can go about this?" Yet even in His moment of weakness and confession, He did not sin because He transitioned into a posture of prayer, humility, and complete surrender to the Father, saying, *"Not as I will, but as You will."*

That is the beauty of having a relationship with the Father. You can be honest and tell it like it is because He already knows what it is. He sees beyond the masks and the facades and He sees you for who you truly are. This truth can be both frightening and comforting, depending on how you receive it. But you can find comfort in knowing that even the worst version of yourself—and even the worst version of the world's greatest criminal—is still considered worthy of God's love and redemptive plan for all humanity.

> *When we were utterly helpless, Christ came at just the right time and died for us sinners. Now, most people would not be willing to die for an upright person, though someone might perhaps be willing to die for a person who is especially good. But God showed his great love for us by sending Christ to die for us while we were still sinners.* (Romans 5:6–8 NLT)

8

THE PRESSURE OF "WHAT'S NEXT"

Now that you understand the beauty of being, how do you do it? How can you live in this perpetual state when you are constantly faced with the pressure of *what's next?* In this chapter, I hope to teach you how to find true contentment and ditch the trap of comparison that is robbing your joy and peace. Because the truth is, God's timing is perfect, and He is in control of your life. He will take care of you, and you don't have to worry or allow the pressures of this world to stress you out. I will share practical tools and habits you can easily use to slow down and find peace in your everyday life. This includes creating systems that leave space for grace and cultivating environments that encourage divine simplicity and intentional living. As daughters of God, it's time to break up with feeling overwhelmed and start living for an audience of One. There is no reason to feel rushed into certain seasons of life, and it's okay to pause before moving on to the *next big thing.* You can find beauty in your journey of *being* while becoming, and in this chapter, you will be encouraged to *breathe* and take actionable steps to grow in gratitude while also implementing journaling techniques, biblical practices, and perspective shifts to unlock a life of true peace and fulfillment.

The first step in this direction is acknowledging that contentment is a state of being that must be *learned*. I myself love to glean from the Bible's example of Paul. He himself explicitly stated on several occasions how he *learned* to be content. Philippians 4:11–13 says:

> *I am not saying this because I am in need, for I have* **learned to be content** *whatever the circumstances. I know what it is to be in need, and I know what it is to have plenty.* **I have learned the secret of being content** *in any and every situation, whether well fed or hungry, whether living in plenty or in want. I can do all this through him who gives me strength.*

LEARNING TO BE CONTENT

There are several takeaways I get from this Scripture:

1. If we are *intentional* and learn how to be content, we can have this state of being no matter what the circumstance.

2. Being content is the *secret* to experiencing a fulfilling life that is anchored by God's peace.

3. *"I can do all things through Christ who strengthens me"* (Philippians 4:13 NKJV) is a verse that is contextually referring to one's endurance. Yet this verse is often wrongly interpreted and misused to promote and justify one's vain ambitions.

If we truly learn how to be content, we will unlock something that I believe not many people truly ever get to experience in life—that is, the beauty of being. So how can you unlock this? How can you learn how to be content and what is the key to this?

The answer is: When the search is over.

The search for truth. The search for peace. The search for meaning and purpose.

We all come into this world looking for those three things. No matter who you are, your soul can't help but search them out. The world refers to this process as *soul-searching*. The Bible refers to it as *seeking*. Many are searching their soul when they should really just be seeking the Lord. The Bible actually has many verses about this process of seeking. The Greek word for *seeking* is *zéteó*, which means "to seek, to search for, to desire, to strive after."[5] Most people have this great desire within them, and they know that they are seeking and striving for something beyond themselves. The truth is, God designed and programmed us all to seek Him so that we might find Him and become saved. This is how God draws us to Himself; He places a longing and desire within each of us so that we might come to know Him.

Jesus says in John 6:44, *"No one can come to me unless the Father who sent me draws them, and I will raise them up at the last day."*

The problem is, many go through life and they feel this tug and drawing from the Lord, but they are deceived and drawn to everyone and everything else but Him. Unfortunately, due to the natural tendencies of the flesh, humans are drawn to sin, drugs, sex, alcohol, perversion, overeating, and all types of things that we think will bring us comfort, numb the pain we experience, or address some other issue. The thing is, there comes a point in our life when we finally get tired of being drawn to the wrong things, and we desire to draw from the well of living water that never runs dry. I am thinking of the story of the Samaritan woman at the well in John 4.

---

5. G2212. *zéteó*. *Strong's Greek Concordance.*

GOD'S GIFT OF LIVING WATER

Jesus met her in that place of drought and desperation, in the middle of the desert. You yourself may feel like you're in a spiritual desert; you keep drawing from the wrong wells and you keep coming up thirsty, wanting more. Jesus had asked the Samaritan woman for a drink, but she was surprised He would ask her this because Jews did not normally associate with Samaritans.

> *Jesus answered her, "If you knew the gift of God and who it is that asks you for a drink, you would have asked him and he would have given you living water." "Sir," the woman said, "you have nothing to draw with and the well is deep. Where can you get this living water? Are you greater than our father Jacob, who gave us the well and drank from it himself, as did also his sons and his livestock?" Jesus answered, "Everyone who drinks this water will be thirsty again, but whoever drinks the water I give them will never thirst. Indeed, the water I give them will become in them a spring of water welling up to eternal life."* (John 4:10–14)

What the Samaritan woman didn't know was that Jesus definitely had something to draw with; He was drawing her unto Himself for salvation, through and by the power of God. This woman did not know that she was having an encounter with God that would change her life forever and make her the first evangelist to ever share the good news in the Bible. Jesus knew that the type of water He provided would lead to everlasting life; it is a well that never runs dry.

Jesus knew of this woman's past and that she had five husbands. She is someone who was on a soul-searching journey, looking for wholeness and contentment through men, but unfortunately always coming up empty. Imagine the level of brokenness and fragmentation from having that many soul ties. Imagine being on a soul-searching journey yet giving up another part of your soul to another toxic relationship every time you lie down with another man who is not truly your husband.

I'm glad she was able to have that encounter with Jesus, to end the perpetual cycle that resulted from constantly feeding the unquenchable desires of the flesh. The flesh, unfortunately, cannot be quenched and keeps you in bondage, but the Spirit brings fullness and freedom in Christ. (See 2 Corinthians 3:17.) That is why it is called the *infilling* of the Holy Spirit. The Holy Spirit has a fullness about Him. Instead of being filled with the lust of the flesh, we can be filled with the Holy Spirit. God takes that hollow part of your soul and that emptiness that you feel, and He fills it with His Spirit and sets you free.

> *Do not get drunk on wine, which leads to debauchery. Instead, be filled with the Spirit.* (Ephesians 5:18)

As we said previously, people are often searching for truth, peace, meaning, and purpose. When your soul is settled with the truth, God's peace, and a clear sense of purpose, you are no longer just living to survive, but you learn to simply *be* and thrive.

CALLED TO THRIVE LIKE A TREE

When someone wants to plant a tree, they consider the land that's available. Then they till the soil, lay down the seeds or plant a little tree, and water the ground. Some species of trees can live thousands of years; the Great Basin bristlecone pine in the western United States can live up to five thousand years. If anyone needs an example of the beauty of *being*, take a look outside at all the beautiful, strong, tall trees. They don't strive to survive; they only thrive. As righteous children of our Father God, we are called to thrive like trees.

That person is like a tree planted by streams of water, which yields its fruit in season and whose leaf does not wither—whatever they do prospers.   (Psalm 1:3)

To be like these righteous trees, we must be planted by the streams, our source, our reservoir—God Himself. We talked about drawing from the well of God's living water. I believe that as righteous trees, this is the best type of water that will have us live even beyond natural trees that live to be five thousand years old, but we will thrive into everlasting life as long as we remain in God.

John 15:4 says, *"Remain in me, as I also remain in you. No branch can bear fruit by itself; it must remain in the vine. Neither can you bear fruit unless you remain in me."*

We must be connected to the source to bear fruit. God is the great vine and we are His branches. The world will tell you that in order to bear fruit and be successful, you have to *go, go, go* and *hustle hard.* But here, God is saying the opposite. He is saying, if you want to be fruit and bear fruit, you must *remain.* You must *rest* in Him. You must settle on this truth, find your spiritual plot of land, and remain right there, plant, water, and grow.

The Greek word and biblical meaning for *remain* is *menó.* It means "to remain, abide, stay, wait."[6] You have to wait for something to grow; you have to wait and see the results over time. But what happens when you are unstable and impatient? What happens when you are easily swayed, pressured, and quick to give up? You cut short the growth process and you miss out on the fruit and harvest that God desires for you.

For example, if you kept planting a tree in different spots, changing your mind about where it should be, digging up its roots and never allowing it to grow, you would never see the fruit of it. If you grew up like me, moving from place to place, going to a new

6. G3306. menó. *Strong's Greek Concordance.*

school almost every year, and dealing with a lot of instability and changes, you might find it hard to find peace and confidence or to truly know yourself at a young age.

That is the enemy's plan. He comes to cause confusion, division, and instability, sow seeds of doubt, break up families, and do whatever else he can to shake your faith. He comes *"to steal and kill and destroy"* (John 10:10).

Mark 4:15 says, *"Some people are like seed along the path, where the word is sown. As soon as they hear it, Satan comes and takes away the word that was sown in them."*

If you keep allowing Satan to steal the seed of God's Word that's been planted in you, you'll miss out on the beauty of being. You'll miss out on growing into that righteous tree that's planted by the streams of water and yields its fruit in season. When you allow God's seeds to be watered in your life, roots will form and stretch deep underground, settling you in the Spirit. It doesn't matter the season or circumstance, as long as God is the One who keeps you grounded, you will be unmovable.

A tree's roots keep it grounded in that spot, that circumstance. But what happens when the environment changes? What happens when circumstances are different? What happens when life hits you with hurricanes and tornadoes that you didn't expect? Can you still be settled and *simply be?* The answer is yes. As long as you remain attached to God, you will be rooted in Him though it may look different in various phases of life and circumstances.

This is because there are so many aspects to God. He is exactly what you need Him to be whenever and wherever. If we are as trees, His truth will be the roots. But what happens if we are no longer on land? What happens when we face the stormy waters of life as boats, being swept away by the waves of this world, dashed against a rocky shore, or capsized and sinking? It's good to know that in any scenario, God's Word will be our anchor. No matter what, the most important thing is to be content and remain in God. Our faith must truly become cemented over time as we grow in the Lord.

James 1:6 (NLT) says, *"But when you ask him, be sure that your faith is in God alone. Do not waver, for a person with divided loyalty **is as unsettled as a wave of the sea** that is blown and tossed by the wind."*

As you see from this verse, a wave is the perfect example of how we should *not* live. We should not be unsettled, moved by every wind of doctrine, easily swayed or easily deceived. God desires for us to be settled in our faith, but in order to do that, we cannot doubt or be divided in our loyalty. You can't serve two masters; you must only serve God. You can't live to please people when you are dedicated to pleasing God. You must rid your life of every idol and make Jesus your number one.

When you settle on His truth, when you rest in His peace, and when you realize His purpose for your life, you will finally start to experience the beauty of being.

As I said in the beginning of this chapter, this process must be learned; it must be done with intention. You have to start saying *yes* to God and saying no to everything else that is competing for your faith, focus, allegiance, peace, and purpose.

OVERCOMING BONDAGE TO SELF

Even when we've mastered the art of saying no to any external pressures imposed upon us, there is still a space for a greater level of freedom to happen. Some of us are our own worst enemies and are in bondage to self. Do you spend all day thinking about yourself, your problems, your life—you, you, you? Do all your prayers start with, "God, can I please have…" or "God, do you think I should do…" or "God, please grow my…"? These are okay prayers. But what if we moved beyond ourselves and prayed prayers like, "God, who can I bless today?" or "God, what can I do to advance Your kingdom's mission on earth?"

You may feel like that pressure is coming from an external factor, but sometimes it is really just from within. We can place pressures, expectations, and constraints on ourselves because we are so consumed with self. For some of us, it's not necessarily that others are rushing us; instead, we sometimes rush ourselves. We place a time limit on God to perform the works that we desire Him to do in our lives. What if, for once, you told yourself *no?* What if, for once, you surveyed your own dreams, hopes, desires, and plans to decide if they are really worth pursuing? What are you willing to lay down in order to follow Jesus? Are you willing to carry your cross and give God your treasures? The things dearest to your heart? The things you love the most?

Recently, I gave God one of my childhood dreams. My dream of being a fashion model had died. I decided to retire from competing in worldly pageants because I feel led to now start a Christian beauty pageant that promotes the values of God. It was hard laying that down, but it was worth it to allow God to reroute me so that He might be number one and He might get the glory. I've had my share of wearing the crowns and holding the pageant titles. From that experience, I have learned that these things are only temporal; they are not eternal. That is why my new Christian beauty pageant is called "Miss Eternity" because it is based on an eternal value system and the fruit of the Spirit.

Charm is deceptive, and beauty is fleeting; but a woman who fears the LORD is to be praised.   (Proverbs 31:30)

THE DEATH OF A CHILDHOOD DREAM

Here is the letter I wrote to my "self" after grieving the death of a childhood dream:

Dear mini-me, right now we are grieving the death of a childhood dream. Satan wants to have you and bury you in the pit of disappointment, but God will pull you out. As a little girl, you were met with the pressures of *becoming*. The former generation asked you, "What do you want to become when you grow up?" As if the beauty of simply being a child was not enough. So you grew up with the goal of becoming a fashion model. You looked to women way beyond your years and desired to grow up too fast, robbing you of parts of the childhood you were supposed to have.

You looked up and out into the world. You saw the top models on the silver screen and began to develop this childhood dream. The glitz, glamour, latest fashions, and pearls enticed you as a little girl. Then when you got saved, you fell into the trap of shame. Though the dream still remained, the vision you once had was no longer your aim. You went from colorful and bright to dull and trying to hide.

Your twenties took you for a ride. You did everything you thought you should, not much of what you really liked. You served in ministry and pleased as many people as you could while your true self tried to hide. So when you turned thirty, God gave you a break. He said, "Have fun" and "Go live your life." The beauty queen rose up on the inside. The childhood dream of becoming a model was revived. God even changed the rules so you could try. No more limits on age; pageant contestants could now be a mom and a wife.

Before you set foot on that stage, the Holy Spirit said, "Give it your all. This is your last time." You walked into the spotlight and had fun; you made it the time of your life. It was a climax, a super high moment in your life. God gave you the chance to shine and do what *you* liked, but once it was over, your dream, now fulfilled, had died.

You are grieving the death of a childhood dream, but it's alright. Some people never even get to try. Now as you grow into the woman God has called you to be, wipe away your tears and leave the childish things behind. Learn the lessons you need to learn so in the next season, you will be free. God will not leave you empty. He still has a plan and a purpose for your life. The night that your dream died, He awakened *His* dream for you inside.

You dream of being a worshipper, a lyricist, making music, writing lines. You dream that next time you step foot on a stage, the glory is all His, not mine. You dream that through your words and sounds of worship, you will touch hearts and change lives. Just don't forget that with this dream, have fun, give it your all, and let God's Spirit be your guide.

> *When I was a child, I spoke as a child, I understood as a child, I thought as a child; but when I became a man, I put away childish things.* (1 Corinthians 13:11 NKJV)

WHEN GOD ASKS US TO SACRIFICE A DREAM

I am not the only one who experienced the fulfillment of a dream only for God to ask for it back on the altar of sacrifice. Perhaps you have experienced this too.

Abraham had been believing God for a son for years. Finally in his old age, his wife Sarah became pregnant with Isaac. Abraham lived to see God's promise manifest in his life, but in Genesis 22, God asks Abraham to sacrifice Isaac, *"your only son, whom you love ... as a burnt offering"* (verse 2). Abraham could have been swayed by the pressure of, "What's next?" He could have been overcome with the need to take matters into his own hands. Instead, he relinquished control and continued on in obedience into his destiny.

Isaac spoke to Abraham his father and said, "My father!"
And he said, "Here I am, my son." Then he said, "Look, the
fire and the wood, but where is the lamb for a burnt offer-
ing?" And Abraham said, "My son, God will provide for
Himself the lamb for a burnt offering." So the two of them
went together.   (Genesis 22:7–8 NKJV)

In that moment, Abraham said *no* to the pressure of *what's*
next in his life as a father. He trusted that God would provide not
only the lamb for the burnt offering but also provide him with purpose and life, which is a result of obedience. I'm sure Abraham
treasured and loved his son, but he didn't treasure Isaac more than
he treasured God. Nor did he even treasure the security of his
future over the Lord.

So what do you treasure? Do you treasure your visions,
dreams, and desires more than God? Do you treasure the idea of
your future and goals more than Him? Or are you willing to lay
down all idols and pick up your cross to follow Him?

This reminds me of the rich young ruler who had a lot of treasure and didn't want to give it up.

Jesus told him, "If you want to be perfect, go and sell all your
possessions and give the money to the poor, and you will have
treasure in heaven. Then come, follow me." But when the
young man heard this, he went away sad, for he had many
possessions.   (Matthew 19:21–22 NLT)

Many of us are carnal-minded, only concerned with the temporary and what's happening next in our own personal life. We
want to know where we will be in life a year from now or a decade
from now. But what if we shifted our perspective to an eternal
perspective? We would move from the pressure of what's next in
this life to the glory of what's to come in eternal life. The reality

of eternity is both terrifying and promising at the same time. Terrifying because when you realize how tiny you are within the span of eternity, you realize just how big God is. Promising because the same big God who created eternity is the same Father who wants to love and carry you through it all.

9

REST, RESET, AND REFRESH

The enemy comes to steal your joy through stress and strife and he wants you to go through life weary and overwhelmed. Yet there is rest for your soul. That's not to say that life will be a walk in the park because trials and tribulations do sometimes come. Still, the yoke that the Lord gives us is easy and His burden is light. (See Matthew 11:30.) As believers, God desires for us to *soar on wings like eagles* (Isaiah 40:31). God promises that He will renew our strength, especially when we feel faint. This happens when you are positioned to rest, reset, and refresh. This chapter will share how to enter this divine dimension and create serene spaces that invite God's peace and presence in your everyday life.

God created different levels and types of rest, just as He created different stages of sleep, from a light stage that occurs just as you fall asleep to the deepest stage of rapid eye movement (REM) in which you dream.

With each stage of sleep, you are getting a deeper level of rest than the previous one. It is the same way spiritually that God has created different types and levels of rest for us to experience.

FIVE STAGES OF REST THAT GOD PROVIDES

I believe that there are five overarching stages of rest that God provides for us:

1. **Level 1: Natural sleep (daily).** All humans experience this stage of rest, which is a gift of God. His Word tells us, *"In peace I will lie down and sleep"* (Psalm 4:8).

2. **Level 2: Sabbath rest (weekly).** This is the type of rest that God modeled for us on the seventh day of creation after all His work was complete. Believers are commanded to enter into *"a Sabbath-rest"* (Hebrews 4:9).

3. **Level 3: Light yoke rest (situational).** This is the type of rest Christ gives you in exchange for any cares, burdens, or worries you may have. (See Matthew 11:28–30.)

4. **Level 4: Peace (ongoing).** You can have peace at all times despite the circumstances. Scripture says, *"You will keep in perfect peace those whose minds are steadfast, because they trust in you"* (Isaiah 26:3).

5. **Level 5: God's rest (eternal).** When we take our last breath, those who are saved will enter into blissful eternal rest. Heaven will be a place where we won't have another care or worry in the world. (See Hebrews 4:10.)

Unfortunately, some people never experience any rest beyond sleep. Only those who walk with God will be able to experience all five stages of God's rest. Those who do not know God go through life without any true peace, and if they die unsaved, they will never have the opportunity to experience the gift of God's eternal rest. One of the reasons I wrote this book, *The Beauty of Being*, is because I realized the utter need for true rest and peace in a world that is constantly promoting striving. I want you to challenge yourself and review all these stages of rest and ask yourself, "Am I truly taking advantage and benefitting from each and every one?"

Personally, I could get better Level 1 rest, which is natural sleep. I don't always get the recommended eight hours and I am a very light sleeper. I have been doing well at Sabbath rest; I make that a priority for me and my family because I see the positive impact it has had on my life, mind, business, ministry, and more. I have also been improving in Level 3 rest because I've grown in my prayer life ever since I started tracking my prayers and operating from a place of childlike faith. I am quick to give my heavy burdens and worries to the Lord and take His light yoke in exchange. I am at complete peace, which is Level 4 rest. I also am ready for Level 5 because I know my eternity is secure in the Lord. So the main thing I need to work on is Level 1 rest.

Your experience may be different. Maybe you sleep well and wake up feeling refreshed, but you want to practice Level 3 rest and cast your cares on the Lord. Wherever you are, that's okay, as long as you recognize and acknowledge that there is a guaranteed level and place of rest that God has for you. Don't allow the enemy to steal the gift of rest and peace from you. It is part of your inheritance as a beloved child of God.

GROUNDS OF REST

Believe it or not, the beginning of our being goes back to our creation from the ground, and there is great significance in this. Genesis 2:7 says, *"Then the LORD God formed a man from the dust of the ground and breathed into his nostrils the breath of life, and the man became a living **being**."* Man is made from God's breath and the dust of the ground. When we are feeling weary and we need to be revived, refreshed, and renewed, we need to return to the core of our original design, for we were created from breath and ground. You need the breath of God to breathe on you again, for it is He who gives you rest. When you feel like you are tired, exhausted, and just need to catch a break or a breath, ask God to breathe on you and be your peace. Man was made from the ground, and when we enter into rest after this life, to the ground we shall return. That is why Genesis 3:19 (NLT) says, *"By the sweat of your brow will you have food to eat until you return to the ground from which you were made. For you were made from dust, and to dust you will return."* While on this earth, there is a level of toil and striving we must endure to survive that came with the fall of man in the garden of Eden. But this toiling won't last always; God says we will eventually return to the ground, but while we are still on this earth living life, He provides grounds of rest. Did you also know that woman was created from the rib of Adam while he was in a deep sleep? (See Genesis 2:21.) Rest was one of the first things God allowed humanity to experience.

I want to talk about the grounds of rest that God provides for us as we navigate through this life and how to recognize those spaces and places that many of us seek. In the Greek, the word ground is *gé*,[7] which means the physical earth, the ground where we live that God uses to prepare us for eternity. Did you know that resting and being plays a role in preparing you for eternity? What a profound revelation. Many of us think that in order to prepare for anything, we need to work hard, try more, or do more. But for eternity, the most important appointment we will ever have, the best way we can enter God's rest is practicing holy rest in Him on this earth.

> *For all who have entered into God's rest have rested from their labors, just as God did after creating the world.*
> (Hebrews 4:10 NLT)

For every level of rest, God sets aside a specific ground for us to settle in, just as a seed must rest and settle into its ground before

7. G1093. gé. *Strong's Greek Concordance.*

its roots can go deep, allowing it to grow and thrive. What kind of ground are you building your life upon and resting on? Is it *"holy ground"* (Exodus 3:5)? Is it *legal ground*—legalistic or words-based living? (See Romans 7:10.) Or is it *"solid ground"* (Psalm 26:12 NLT)? I want to rest on God's holy ground. I want to rest on God's solid ground. I don't want to build my foundation on the law. I don't want to build my foundation on words and performance. I want to build my life on God's grounds of rest.

For each level of rest from 1 to 5—sleep, sabbath, situational, internal peace, and eternal bliss—God also provides a ground and space for us to be planted and thrive in. For example, the ground for Level 1, of course, would be a bed. For Level 2, it might be sitting on a couch or church pew. For Level 3, it is a prayer closet. For Level 4, it is the comfort of the Holy Spirit. For Level 5, it's beyond the grave, for it is heaven itself. In every single level and stage of rest, God is there to comfort us in some way or another. He is always faithful to provides grounds for rest.

> *And I will pray the Father, and He will give you another [Comforter], that He may abide with you forever.*
> (John 14:16 NKJV)

The more you are rested on the grounds set aside for you at every stage, the more that you experience the beauty of being. Let me further explain by giving you a few more practical examples of what I mean, and then we will go into spiritual aspects of rest.

When you are ready to settle down and start a family, you spend time, maybe even years, searching for the perfect home and plot of land, a physical house to lay your roots and raise your family. Then when you decide on the grounds, you move into that house and it becomes your place of rest. That is how a house becomes a home.

To give you another example, when someone passes away and enters into an eternal state of rest, their family members may search out a plot of land for their gravesite if the deceased hasn't selected one before passing. They will find a plot of land to settle the casket into the ground, and then the land becomes a grave. But when the deceased transitions into glory, what was once a grave becomes a door into God's rest and their eternal home.

The greatest level of rest that we can experience on this earth is Level 4, God's peace. Peace is actually a fruit of the Spirit. (See Galatians 5:22.) God is saying, *"Peace, be still"* (Mark 4:39 NKJV) as Jesus did when He calmed the storm and raging waters. That is the command of the Lord. Where there is no peace, there is chaos, anxiety, worry, and fear. Maybe you feel like that on the inside, your soul is like a raging storm with tempest waves. Perhaps you have brain fog and are easily distracted and forgetful. Or you may feel like you're all over the place. This often happens when we are battling our inner demons, restless and constantly struggling with mental strongholds. Just know this is not your portion nor is it God's desire for you. Instead of the tempest waves, God wants to give you still waters. In exchange for anxiety, God wants to give you peace. Instead of chaos and bondage, God wants you to thrive in His order and be free.

Philippians 4:6–7 says, *"Do not be anxious about anything, but in every situation, by prayer and petition, with thanksgiving, present your requests to God. And the peace of God, which transcends all understanding, will guard your hearts and your minds in Christ Jesus."*

RESTING IN GOD'S PERFECT PEACE

Resting in God's perfect peace is essential to the beauty of being. In His peace, we hear the still, small voice of the Holy Spirit more clearly and accurately. (See 1 Kings 19:12.) In His peace, we get to witness Him move and experience a greater dimension of His glory. His peace is what guides us along the right, narrow path.

An old hymn features the lyrics, "I've got peace like a river ... I've got peace like a river in my soul."[8] In normal instances, when the weather is fine, a river flows calmly within a channel of defined banks. The banks act as boundaries of land, directing the river through the channel and guiding the water into a sea, lake, or ocean. Just like a river is set up with boundaries to guide it along a certain path, God uses His peace as a way to discipline us, protect us, lead us, and guide us. His Word tells us:

Peace I leave with you; my peace I give you. I do not give to you as the world gives. Do not let your hearts be troubled and do not be afraid. (John 14:27)

He lets me rest in green meadows; he leads me beside peaceful streams. He renews my strength. He guides me along right paths, bringing honor to his name. (Psalm 23:2–3 NLT)

We can learn a lot from how rivers flow along a given path. When we follow the boundaries God has set for our lives, we are connected to His peace. It keeps us refreshed, nourishes our spirit-man, and causes the fruit of the Spirit to take root and produce fruit in our lives. God always wants us to stay connected to His peace.

The refrain for another popular hymn says, "On Christ the solid rock I stand; all other ground is sinking sand."[9] Sometimes we are going through life overwhelmed, feeling buried by the cares, pressures, and stressors of this world, and we are literally sinking under it all, because we are not rooted and rested on the right ground. I want to remind you that Christ is the solid rock on which you can stand. He is your solid ground of rest. All other ground is sinking sand! We are called to build our life on the rock and solid ground of Christ.

---

8. Trad., "Peace Like a River," 1800s.
9. Edward Mote, "My Hope Is Built on Nothing Less," 1834.

> *Whoever hears these sayings of Mine, and does them, I will liken him to a wise man who built his house on the rock: and the rain descended, the floods came, and the winds blew and beat on that house; and it did not fall, for it was founded on the rock. But everyone who hears these sayings of Mine, and does not do them, will be like a foolish man who built his house on the sand: and the rain descended, the floods came, and the winds blew and beat on that house; and it fell. And great was its fall.* (Matthew 7:24–27 NKJV)

The words you hear, believe, and receive are directly correlated to the ground you are building on spiritually. This previous Scripture shows that if we are hearing God's Word of truth and applying it to our life, we are building our house on a rock. The situations of life can't change that because we still have that situational peace He provides for us at Level 3. We don't have to feel intimidated when the floods and the winds come. But if we do not receive God's words of truth and we allow the world's words and society's words to be our foundation, that is like building our house on sinking sand. Don't listen to the world, which says you are defined by your status, looks, and bank account. Don't listen to society, which says you are validated by your popularity or performance. Listen to God's Word that says, *"We are more than conquerors through him who loved us"* (Romans 8:37). Listen to God's Word that says you are *"more precious than rubies"* (Proverbs 3:15). Listen to God's Word that says, *"To live is Christ and to die is gain"* (Philippians 1:21). The Word of the Lord will give you faith to believe and the peace to rest in what you know. It is the seed we need to thrive in every area of life. For *"faith comes by hearing, and hearing by the word of God"* (Romans 10:17 NKJV).

I truly believe that people lack peace because they lack faith. If you don't truly believe what you say you believe, or it is only head knowledge, you won't be moved to apply what you know to your life, and it won't have the power to change you. If you truly have faith and believe that God is who He says He is, that He will do what He said He would do, and that His promises are *yes* and *amen*, it gives you this deep and great sense of peace that no man can ever take away. Peace is the stillness that comes when we believe.

When you have peace, even the stormy waves that you think are designed to drown you can actually be the ground where you stand as long as God is with you. Did you hear that? *Yes*, when God is with you, even water can be a ground of peace. In Matthew 14:25, Jesus walked on water out to the disciples, who were in a boat on a lake.

> *When the disciples saw him walking on the lake, they were terrified. "It's a ghost," they said, and cried out in fear. But Jesus immediately said to them: "Take courage! It is I. Don't be afraid."*   (Matthew 14:26–27)

You see, fear is the one thing that hinders our peace. Rather than recognizing Jesus and realizing something supernatural had happened, their minds were consumed with fear and assumed something paranormal was occurring. They thought they had seen a ghost. Jesus told them to take courage. He did not want them to be overwhelmed with fear. Then Jesus called Peter to come out of the boat to meet him, and Peter started to walk on the water toward Jesus. As long as his eyes were on Jesus, the water was Peter's solid ground of peace in that moment, but when he saw the wind, he became afraid and immediately began to sink. (See Matthew 14:29–30.) It is always when we take our eyes off the Lord that we become overwhelmed with fear and start to drown in life. Verse 31 says, *"Immediately Jesus reached out his hand and caught him. 'You of little faith,' he said, 'why did you doubt?'"* Doubt and a lack of faith are detrimental to your peace. They try to rob you of experiencing the beauty of being in the Lord.

I'm also reminded of the time Jesus calmed a storm. In Luke 8:22–25, the disciples were in a boat on the lake when a storm came up. *"The boat was being swamped, and they were in great danger"* (verse 23), but Jesus was asleep; He had entered deep Level 1 rest.

> *The disciples went and woke him, saying, "Master, Master, we're going to drown!" He got up and rebuked the wind and the raging waters; the storm subsided, and all was calm. "Where is your faith?" he asked his disciples.*
>
> (Luke 8:24–25)

This further proves the point that your peace is directly connected to your faith. Jesus had peace to the point of sleeping during the storm, but the disciples lacked faith and instead of peace, they were overwhelmed with fear. Jesus said to the storm and the sea, *"Peace, be still!"* (Mark 4:39 NKJV). The disciples were amazed that even the winds and waves obeyed Him. I want to encourage you today that the winds, waters, and waves of your life must submit to the word of peace from your heavenly Father. You do not have to drown, nor should you be overwhelmed.

> *This is my command—be strong and courageous! Do not be afraid or discouraged. For the LORD your God is with you wherever you go.*   (Joshua 1:9 NLT)

Recently, I experienced an extreme sense of peace when I visited a day spa in celebration of my best friend's birthday. During that experience, God truly ministered to me concerning peace.

As my masseuse lifted my arms and exfoliated my skin, she told me, "Just let go." I realized I was subconsciously pulling my weight and raising my arms with my own strength. The masseuse could feel my tense energy and just wanted me to relax. Her job requires her to facilitate a comforting and calming experience. The atmosphere was set with serene music, aromatic scents, and breathtaking scenery. Still, even with this perfectly staged environment, I had to be intentional about letting go.

That is how it is with some of us and our relationship with God. The Holy Spirit is referred to in the Bible as a *Comforter*. In God's intent to comfort us, He provides the perfect design for us to experience divine support and serenity as we are here on this earth. Just as my environment was intentionally curated at the spa, our lives as children of God are orchestrated to give us a full experience. You were meant to go through life thriving, not merely surviving. Jesus came so that you could have life more abundantly.

John 10:10 (NLT) says, "*The thief's purpose is to steal and kill and destroy. My purpose is to give them a rich and satisfying life.*"

I didn't go to the spa that day because I *needed* to. I went because I *wanted* to. I wanted to experience the satisfaction of a relaxing spa day massage and believe it or not, there was still *purpose* in it. From the Scripture verse above, we see that Jesus is declaring that there is *purpose* for a life that is pleasurable, satisfying, and full of rich experiences.

Many times in the church, we have been taught that purpose is only related to pain and duty. That is why when we talk about purpose, we often use verbiage surrounding what we *need* to do or what we are *called* to do rather than what we *get* to experience or *find joy* in doing. Some of us even go to the extreme of condemning all pleasure and assuming that any desires we have must be rooted in sin or the lust of the flesh. But the truth is, when we delight ourselves in God, He gives us the desires of our hearts. (See Psalm 37:4.)

I did not *need* to go to the spa. My body was not in pain and I did not feel called to witness to my masseuse. Although these would have been great reasons for my spa visit and would have served a good purpose, my desire to simply go and enjoy a spa day was already purposeful within itself.

If this teaching is making you uncomfortable, or if you sometimes feel guilty for having a little clean fun in life, I want to ask you this: Is God not a *good* Father who gives good gifts to His children as Matthew 7:11 tells us? Is God not the Creator of all things *"for His good pleasure"* (Philippians 2:13 NKJV)? Have we not been created in His image and likeness? (See Genesis 1:27.)

If the God of the universe created things for pleasure and if we are made in His own image, don't you think He would like us to experience pleasure as He does? If not, why did He give us our senses? Why did He give us taste buds to taste delicious food? Why did God give us nostrils to smell the amazing flowers and scents? If God did not delight in us having pleasure, why did He give us eyes to see the beautiful wonders of His creation? Why did He give us senses to experience touch and feeling as I experienced during my amazing massage at the spa? Pleasure and all these senses are part of God's plan to have us experience the abundant life that He designed for us to have. That is the beauty of simply being, living, feeling, and experiencing, all for the glory of God.

Too many Christians are walking around moping and complaining about life. It is as if we are expected to live a miserable downtrodden life of faith 24/7. If that is the case, why would anyone desire the life that we have? We are called to be *"the light of the world"* (Matthew 5:14). We are called to provide hope to a dark and dying world because when others see us, they should see the Holy Spirit's fullness of life and joy reflected in us. People should see us and say, "I want to know what's different about that person. I want the joy that they have. I want the peace that they have."

The problem is, many of us are not able to open our hands to receive what the Comforter has in store for us because we are too busy trying to lift our own weight. Spiritually, our hands are carrying all the things that we should have dropped long ago.

What are you still holding on to? What is weighing you down that you need to let go of? Is it unforgiveness from a person who hurt you? Is it disappointment and regret from past seasons? Or is it control and your inability to trust the Lord?

Whatever it is, I encourage you to let go of it today. Picture yourself lying on the bed of God's heavenly spa and hearing the Good Shepherd say, *"Take My yoke upon you and learn from Me, for I am gentle and lowly in heart, and you will find rest for your souls. For My yoke is easy and My burden is light"* (Matthew 11:29–30 NKJV).

I just want this to serve as a reminder that you don't have to support yourself through life. Just as I had made the mistake of trying to lift my own weight at the spa, God wants you to trust that He is providing you with His perfect support system and plan for your life. God's perfect spa design for your life is made up of several components to make sure you leave this world relaxed, refreshed, and ready to enter His eternal rest:

+ The Sabbath bed of rest (Exodus 20:8)
+ The shower of the Word (Ephesians 5:26)
+ The still waters of refreshment (Psalm 23:2–3)
+ The sauna of refinement (Malachi 3:2)

We can be in the presence of the Holy Spirit, be active in our local church body, and have the perfect environment, community, and support system surrounding us, but still be unwilling to let go and simply *be*. A great way to be intentional about this is mastering the art of slowing down. Did you know that there is a wrong and right way to slow down? I recognized this the other day, and it's all dependent on your posture.

If you slow down from a posture of fear, it's not leading to rest, but rather it's leading to stress. On the other hand, if you slow down from a place of faith, it's putting you in a place of true rest and peace.

I want to share with you two different scenarios of how it looks to slow down the wrong way versus the right way.

SLOWING DOWN THE WRONG WAY

You are at a party with friends and family. You slow down by spending fifteen minutes trying to capture the perfect selfie of yourself and then you proceed to post the photo on social media. You grab a bite of food to eat, scarf it down, and step into a separate room to take a nap.

SLOWING DOWN THE RIGHT WAY

You are at a party with friends and family. You pause for a moment to take a family photo to memorialize the occasion, and then you continue to spend quality time with your loved ones. You say grace over the food and eat it mindfully while having a conversation with your family. You thank the person who made the food and take a moment to sit down and digest it before enjoying a small piece of dessert.

In the first example, slowing down the wrong way causes you to lose precious time. It also isolates you and robs you of simple joys. In the second example, slowing down the right way causes you to cherish precious time. It puts you in community and helps you appreciate and find joy in the little things. Slowing down the wrong way is really just time mismanagement. It's wasting time on trivial things and missing out on pockets of joy that are hidden in the day. It's not spending enough time on what matters; precious time is lost due to outside distractions and self-absorption. I think we can all do a better job at being more intentional and slowing down the right way.

The other day, I baked and decorated my first three-tier cake for my daughters and I enjoyed every moment of the process. It caused me to focus and slow down, and that's one of the things that I really enjoy about the hobby of baking. The focus, creativity, and attention to detail that it requires gives me a moment to embrace the beauty of being. It was an opportunity to think deeply about why I was baking the cake, how much my daughters mean to me, the precious memories I have of them, and so on. This is how I believe life is supposed to be lived—not rushed but truly enjoyed.

> *So I saw that there is nothing better for a person than to enjoy their work, because that is their lot. For who can bring them to see what will happen after them?* (Ecclesiastes 3:22)

Tomorrow is not promised. We may not be here to see what the future holds or witness the next generation, so we should enjoy ourselves while we are here on this earth. Too many people are going through life simply trying to get by, living from paycheck to paycheck, truly stuck in a rat race, and never stopping to smell the roses.

You can never get back any time that is lost. That is why it's important to cherish the time you have and not waste it trying to keep up with the Joneses or pleasing other people. What is the point of looking like your life is enjoyable when you're truly not happy and just trying to keep up with a facade?

I hope that my words have encouraged you to break free from the performance mindset and truly experience the pleasure of living free in the Lord.

10

I LAY DOWN MY CROWNS

Maybe you've heard the message, "God is a King, so you are a princess, and that makes you royalty." This is indeed true, and books and sermons have been written about this concept. The problem is, these messages usually only go as far as revealing *you*—*your* royal position, *your* God-given authority, and *your* greatness. The focus of this great revelation is often on *self*. The truth is your royal position was never just about you. Our role as God's daughters is to reflect *His* glory. Any honors that have been bestowed upon us are for God's glory and worship. You were never supposed to look to the titles and the crowns for confidence. When you are rooted within the confidence that comes through Christ alone, the crown is simply an adornment. We are *just* daughters, and that is just enough. Any crown we receive is like icing on the cake for God to enjoy.

You may have the honor and title of being a sister, a wife, a mom, a minister, or something else. Those things are great, but we must realize that God has bestowed honor upon us for His glory. Then when we go on to glory and receive our crowns and rewards at the judgment seat of Christ, it won't be so we can boast, but rather so we can lay down our crowns at His feet as a form of worship and glory unto the King of Kings and Lord of Lords.

We are able to receive eternal crowns that are far more precious than any earthly crown, possession, or treasure.

The Bible says in Matthew 6:19–20 (NLT), "*Don't store up treasures here on earth, where moths eat them and rust destroys them, and where thieves break in and steal. Store your treasures in heaven, where moths and rust cannot destroy, and thieves do not break in and steal.*"

The things that God truly treasures are the things that we too should value. The world tells us to treasure riches, status, influence, and accomplishments. I think that many people would be surprised to learn that a lot of what we deem successful on earth will not be considered important in heaven.

In the Bible, there are five eternal crowns that we are able to earn after this life:

THE CROWN OF REJOICING

For what is our hope, or joy, or crown of rejoicing? Is it not even you in the presence of our Lord Jesus Christ at His coming?   (1 Thessalonians 2:19 NKJV)

The crown of rejoicing comes from truly having your hope and joy placed on the Lord Christ Jesus throughout this life. Your hope can't be in this world. You must know that your joy comes from the Lord and not be consumed with the world's false idol of happiness. People idolize society's concept of happiness because they lack true joy. They will intentionally sin and go to so many lengths just to be happy.

But when you truly have the joy of the Lord, the world cannot take it away. The crown of rejoicing is for those who are thankful and overflowing with gratitude because of the Lord's goodness. They have not let comparison to others affect their joy. They hope because of what they know and believe. They look forward to the return of Christ, and they give Him the worship, glory, honor, and praise due His name.

THE CROWN OF RIGHTEOUSNESS

And now the prize awaits me—the crown of righteousness, which the Lord, the righteous Judge, will give me on the day of his return. And the prize is not just for me but for all who eagerly look forward to his appearing.
(2 Timothy 4:8 NLT)

The crown of righteousness is for those who eagerly look to the return and glorification of Christ. Their focus is not on this world and its temporal pleasures; their focus is on eternity. They love what God loves and hate what God hates. Their hearts and lives have been transformed through the blood of the Lamb. They are the righteousness of God in Christ. They have made Christ not just their Savior but Lord of their life. They have carried their own cross and their life has been poured out as an offering unto God.

THE CROWN OF LIFE

Don't be afraid of what you are about to suffer. The devil will throw some of you into prison to test you. You will suffer for ten days. But if you remain faithful even when facing death, I will give you the crown of life. (Revelation 2:10 NLT)

The crown of life is for those who endure a greater level of persecution on this earth. It's more than just others not liking them or rejecting them. Their persecution can be to the point of death. The ones who receive the crown of life include those who have been thrown into prison yet still endured and kept their faith in the Lord. They refuse to deny Him in hard times and are willing to become martyrs for the faith. They are willing to lose their earthly lives because they know an even better heavenly life awaits.

THE CROWN OF GLORY

> *And when the Great Shepherd appears, you will receive a crown of never-ending glory and honor.*   (1 Peter 5:4 NLT)

The crown of glory will be given to the pastors, shepherds, and servants of God who have been faithfully taking care of God's sheep on His earth while He is away. If you are a pastor or someone in ministry who has grown weary, or maybe even overwhelmed with the burdens you carry because of the role you play in the lives of others, know that there is a crown for you. Just remain faithful and don't give up. God sees how you have dedicated your life to this call and He has a crown of glory awaiting you.

I hope this verse encourages you:

> *So let's not get tired of doing what is good. At just the right time we will reap a harvest of blessing if we don't give up.*
> (Galatians 6:9 NLT)

THE IMPERISHABLE CROWN

> *Everyone who competes in the games goes into strict training. They do it to get a crown that will not last, but we do it to get a crown that will last forever.*   (1 Corinthians 9:25)

The imperishable crown is for those who have let *"patience have its perfect work"* in them (James 1:4 NKJV). It is for the child of God who has endured and has been molded and shaped by the loving discipline of the Father. It is for the one who has been tested and refined through the fire. The imperishable crown is given to those who have constantly denied and resisted the flesh so that the Spirit of God within them might live. They have spiritual fruit to show as a result of their walk with Christ. Their value and experience goes beyond this life. They have concerned themselves with the things of the Spirit and they have truly stored up for themselves treasures in heaven.

DEEP INTIMACY AND WALKING WITH THE LORD

When you look at these crowns, each and every one of them comes from a place of deep intimacy and walking with the Lord. The crowns come from trusting God, obeying God, placing your hope in God, living for God, and serving God. It's all about God. The sad thing is many believers are unfamiliar with these crowns, and they don't even realize that God has already set a standard and given us goals that we can strive for.

Many of us are too busy setting our own goals, our own agendas, and chasing the worldly crowns. Many of us are so consumed with how other people are judging us, or the world's perception of us, that we are not truly cognizant that one day, we will stand before the judgment seat of Christ. Second Corinthians 5:10 says, *"For we must all appear before the judgment seat of Christ, so that each of us may receive what is due us for the things done while in the body, whether good or bad."* Rewards will be given, crowns will be given, but judgments will also be made based on the life that we lived. Everything will come to light, and the motives of our hearts and our intentions will be made public for everyone to see. People may live in sin and use the excuse, "Well, God knows my heart." Yes, He does but that should concern you. Even more alarming, one day, God won't be the only one to know your heart. One day your heart and thoughts will be revealed for all to see. God *"will bring to light what is hidden in darkness"* (1 Corinthians 4:5).

I don't say this to scare you, but to truly give you a perspective shift of what truly matters during this life. We must set aside the carnal and temporal and focus on the spiritual and eternal. That does not mean you have to be a person who goes around preaching fire and brimstone, but you need to have an awareness of the spirit realm and seek constant communication with the Father. You should not be easily drawn or swayed by things that are shallow, superficial, or carnal.

I want to share with you some practical ways that you can set some spiritual and eternal goals, if you haven't already, instead of just focusing on temporal ones.

We are often encouraged to focus on earthly goals, especially when we are asked questions such as, "What do you do?" or "What are you going to major in?" or "Do you have a business?" or "How much money do you want to make?"

Imagine if instead, we were challenged with questions like, "What Scripture is helping you walk through this season of life right now?" or "What spiritual gift or spiritual fruit is God currently cultivating in your life?" or "What is your vision to carry out God's purpose on this earth?"

Unfortunately, those are not the type of questions we are commonly asked, so those are not the areas of life that we typically focus on. Colossians 3:1–2 says, *"Since, then, you have been raised with Christ, set your hearts on things above, where Christ is, seated at the right hand of God. Set your minds on things above, not on earthly things."*

TIPS TO FOCUS ON ETERNAL REWARDS

Here are some practical tips for focusing on eternal rewards rather than earthly ones:

1. *Set the tone of your days with prayer and live in a posture of expectation.*

Let your expectations be on God, not on people, places, or things. How do you expect God to show up in your life? Psalm 5:3 (NLT) says, *"Listen to my voice in the morning, LORD. Each morning I bring my requests to you and wait expectantly."*

When we exercise our faith by placing our expectations on God and patiently wait on Him, we make sure our hope is in God and not in this world.

2. *Perform regular heart checks.*

Our heart is the thing that often gets us in trouble. We should pay close attention to the motives and intentions of our hearts to make sure that they are pleasing to the Lord and not tainted by the world. Pray and ask God if there is anything in your heart displeasing to Him.

Search me, God, and know my heart; test me and know my anxious thoughts. See if there is any offensive way in me, and lead me in the way everlasting. (Psalm 139:23–24)

3. *Make an assessment of your priorities.*

What you spend your time, attention, and money on is what you value. Make an assessment of your priorities. Are you focusing on the right things and do they have an appropriate place in your life? Or are there any idols that you need to repent of and get rid of in your life? Is God truly number one in your life?

But seek first his kingdom and his righteousness, and all these things will be given to you as well. (Matthew 6:33)

Jesus replied: "Love the Lord your God with all your heart and with all your soul and with all your mind."

(Matthew 22:37)

In summary, if you can place your hope and expectation on God, keep your heart in check, and keep Him first in everything you do, this is the most practical way to keep your focus on eternity.

WHAT GOD VALUES

Remember, God does not value the same thing that the world values. God values our character. He values a pure heart and pure intentions. He values our worship, praise, and faithfulness to Him. Jesus outlines the types of characteristics that the Lord values in the Beatitudes, given during His Sermon on the Mount:

Blessed are the poor in spirit, for theirs is the kingdom of heaven. Blessed are those who mourn, for they will be comforted. Blessed are the meek, for they will inherit the earth. Blessed are those who hunger and thirst for righteousness, for they will be filled. Blessed are the merciful, for they will be shown mercy. Blessed are the pure in heart, for they will see God. Blessed are the peacemakers, for they will be called children of God. Blessed are those who are persecuted because of righteousness, for theirs is the kingdom of heaven. Blessed are you when people insult you, persecute you and falsely say all kinds of evil against you because of me. Rejoice and be glad, because great is your reward in heaven, for in the same way they persecuted the prophets who were before you.

(Matthew 5:3–12)

The character traits that we see praised in the Beatitudes are completely different from those praised by the world. Instead of being poor in spirit, the world encourages boastfulness and pride.

Instead of mourning and suffering, the world promotes pursuing the idol of happiness at all costs. We can go down the whole list of the Beatitudes and talk about how these traits are in direct contrast to what the world celebrates and promotes.

It's important to realize that we can't take any of our earthly crowns with us to heaven. Our earthly rewards, medals, trophies, accolades, and degrees won't be worth a thing. You also won't be able to give the rewards as a form of worship to God in heaven, in the same way that you can lay down the crowns you receive as you worship the Father. What you *can* do is commit to giving God the glory as you are on this earth, right here and right now, every day of your life.

POINT OTHERS TO CHRIST

If God graces you to carry out a calling or be in a certain position and people are impressed with you, use that as an opportunity to point them to Christ. If people ask you how you are able to do something, let them know where your help comes from.

I have experienced some great success in different areas of my life, but I would be a fool to think that any of it was on my own accord. I have had people ask me, "How do you do it? How do you balance being a mom, wife, and business owner?" And I always have to respond that it's only by the grace of God. Sometimes I even pause to explain that things are not as perfect as they seem. Let's be real, I don't always get it right. Sometimes I'm so exhausted that I leave the dishes in the sink overnight, or I don't feel like cooking and I just order some fast food. I am far from perfect, but I'm okay with that.

People have even asked me, "How were you able to give birth to four children naturally, without an epidural?" I could do it because the Lord is my strength. Even though the labor pain hurt, I just chose to believe that He designed my body to do what it did. But believe me, if it wasn't for the Lord, my labor and delivery worship playlist, and the fact that God answered my prayers and granted me the grace to have super quick labors, I don't know if I would have been able to hang on any longer. God granted me my heart's desires and answered my prayers, but it was only because of His goodness and grace. I was just the vessel that He decided to bless in those moments. In everything, we should give God glory. Let people know that all the glory belongs to God.

> *Now all glory to God, who is able, through his mighty power at work within us, to accomplish infinitely more than we might ask or think. Glory to him in the church and in Christ Jesus through all generations forever and ever! Amen.*
> (Ephesians 3:20–21 NLT)

As a daughter of God, I am no longer striving to become, perform, or find my identity in anything outside of God. I have found peace and contentment in simply being a daughter of God and allowing Him to get the glory out of my life. It gives me a sense of peace knowing that I don't have to be perfect because in the areas where I am weak, He is strong.

> *But he said to me, "My grace is sufficient for you, for my power is made perfect in weakness." Therefore I will boast all the more gladly about my weaknesses, so that Christ's power may rest on me. That is why, for Christ's sake, I delight in weaknesses, in insults, in hardships, in persecutions, in difficulties. For when I am weak, then I am strong.*
> (2 Corinthians 12:9–10)

I am enjoying the beauty of life and embracing every moment, authentically as the woman God has created me to be, the good and the bad, the ups and the downs. I am free from the opinions of man, I am free from fear, and I am free from the bondage of sin. I am free, free to simply be and live life, and that *"more abundantly"* (John 10:10 NKJV).

My hope is to one day receive a heavenly crown so that I may have the overwhelming pleasure to honor Christ in worship and lay it down at the Master's feet.

CONCLUSION: AN OPEN HEAVEN

Wow, I thought I was finished writing this book, but God is not done with me yet. The night that I completed the final chapter, I experienced an open heaven for the first time, and the Spirit of God came to pay me a sweet visit. I am still in awe of Him. I spent three hours in prayer, from 9 p.m. until the midnight hour. I can feel the presence of God in my room. I could literally see the light surrounding me. Mind you, I was in a dark room, with absolutely no lights on. The atmosphere was charged with worship and prayer, and I know that in that moment, everything I asked God for was *yes* and *amen*. Then my fire alarm went off in my room, literally, but there was no natural fire. I believe it was the presence of God and particles from the cloud of glory that set off the fire alarm.

After a minute, the alarm ringing stopped, and my husband asked me what happened. I told him, "God was here; He came to visit."

During God's visit, He confirmed to me that the messages and revelations written in this book are from His Spirit. They are not of me, and I cannot take the credit for this book. This book is all about Him and all glory belongs to Him and Him alone, and I would not dare take it away.

Thank You, heavenly Father, for visiting me tonight, and thank You for confirming Your word to me. Thank You for allowing me to see the glory of Your presence and for the open heaven that You have opened over me through this book. I ask, Lord, that You would allow this book to carry Your glory and anointing to the nations. That everyone who picks up this book to read it will be hit with Your presence and experience the outpouring of Your blessings in every area of their lives. May this book be a key to open portals in Your presence and bring us from glory to glory in You. It's in your precious Son Jesus's name that we pray. Amen.

ABOUT THE AUTHOR

Karolyne Roberts is a best-selling author and speaker who is blazing the trail for change-makers and transformational leaders around the globe. Through her YouTube channel, she impacts and inspires over 438,000 subscribers worldwide.

Karolyne has been married to her college sweetheart, Kal Roberts, for twelve years and is the mom to their four children. Together they serve faithfully as leaders in their local church and are cofounders of Miss Eternity (misseternity.com), a Christian pageant system dedicated to empowering women through godly confidence coaching, mentorship, leadership development, and discipleship.

Karolyne's women's ministry, Dear Daddy (deardaddy.com), was created for women to embrace their God-given identity as daughters of the King and grow in intimacy with the Father through journaling, prayer, and a lifestyle of worship. Karolyne is also the founder and CEO of the Writers Retreat (writersretreat. com), where she helps believers use their voice and writing to make an impact for the kingdom. In her spare time, Karolyne likes to bake, do at-home facials, swim, and journal.

Welcome to Our House!

We Have a Special Gift for You

It is our privilege and pleasure to share in your love of Christian books. We are committed to bringing you authors and books that feed, challenge, and enrich your faith.

To show our appreciation, we invite you to sign up to receive a specially selected **Reader Appreciation Gift**, with our compliments. Just go to the Web address at the bottom of this page.

God bless you as you seek a deeper walk with Him!

WE HAVE A GIFT FOR YOU. VISIT:

whpub.me/nonfictionthx

WHITAKER
HOUSE